Fakenham-Lancaster and its region

by

E.M. Bridges

B.Sc, M.Sc, Ph.D. FRGS

Larks Press in association with E.M.Bridges and
the Fakenham Museum
of
Gas and Local History

Published by the Larks Press
Ordnance Farmhouse, Guist Bottom, Dereham NR20 5PF
01328 829207
Larks.Press@btinternet.com www.booksatlarkspress.co.uk

in association with E. M. Bridges and
the Fakenham Museum of Gas and Local History

Printed in Great Britain by the MPG Books Group,
Bodmin and King's Lynn

British Library Cataloguing-in-Publication Data
A catalogue record for this book is available
from the British Library

Fakenham-Lancaster

Sponsored by
Fakenham Town Council

and
The Rotary Club of Fakenham

Acknowledgements

The author acknowledges with thanks the practical help and advice freely given by Mr J. Baldwin, of the Fakenham Local History Society.

Mrs Susan Yaxley of Larks Press is thanked for providing editorial advice throughout the preparation of the manuscript.

Mr T. Ashwin is thanked for permission to use excerpts of maps from An Historic Atlas of Norfolk, published by Phillimore, Chichester.

Fakenham Town Council, through its Market Tolls fund, has kindly made a grant available to the Museum to assist with preliminary work for the publication of this book. Mrs J. Perfect, Town Clerk, is thanked for her help in this project.

The Rotary Club of Fakenham has given a grant towards the cost of editing and preparation of illustrations in readiness for printing.

Finally I would like to thank the many individuals, friends, members of the Fakenham Local History Society and Fakenham Museum who have helped, directly or indirectly, in the compilation of this volume.

Contents

Illustrations

Foreword

At the present time, there is no comprehensive reference book which describes the town of Fakenham and its local region. The following pages are an attempt to rectify this omission. During the past century it has been the practice for any city which hosted the annual British Association for the Advancement of Science to produce a learned account of that city and its region. Thus, in 1961 Norwich produced Norwich and its Region, in 1956 Sheffield produced Sheffield and its Region, in 1966 Nottingham produced Nottingham and its Region and in 1971 Swansea produced Swansea and its Region. It was my privilege to be able to contribute to the two latter books in my capacity as an academic and research scientist. The format of these volumes can act as a template for this volume as Fakenham is a local centre for a large area of North Norfolk.

In terms of its physical geography, North Norfolk has limited exposures of the underlying geology. Its relief is not impressive but beneath this unassuming landscape lies comprehensive evidence for the ice ages which affected northern Europe. For this geological record North Norfolk is world famous. Such mundane things as soils underlie the agricultural development of the region: the varied wildlife has resulted in the creation of several nature reserves and the river Wensum is a site of special scientific interest.

Fakenham is neither a city, nor a university town, but for centuries it has performed the functions of a much larger settlement in respect of the surrounding villages. Therefore, it is appropriate that this account should refer also to the surrounding countryside and villages. Sadly, in recent years many civic functions have been taken away as society generally has changed. The impact of supermarkets has changed the nature and scope of the local shopping facilities offered. Nevertheless, Fakenham's shops and traders still make every Thursday a day when the town really comes to life - and some true accents of Norfolk can be heard.

The surrounding countryside bears the mark of many historical changes which may be interpreted from place-names and field patterns as well as from known historical references. Numerous ruined churches are a feature of this part of Norfolk indicating changing fortunes during the medieval period. In more recent times, the history of the area has been shaped by the great estates which surround Fakenham. The names of Coke at Holkham, Townshend at Raynham and Walpole at Houghton are family names which led Norfolk's agricultural and political life in the 18th and 19th centuries.

Norfolk may be an agricultural county, but that does not mean that it has no industries. Admittedly, most industrial activities grew out of the support given to the agricultural base upon which the prosperity of the county and its inhabitants is founded, but some surprising enterprises have grown up, prospered and then faded away. The coming of the railways and, latterly, bus services and the private motor car have opened an era of greater physical and social mobility. This is particularly seen in the changes in Fakenham since the end of the Second World War. At the end of the first decade of the 21st century it is interesting to look both back and forward and to speculate what Fakenham may be like in the future.

Previously, several aspects of life in Fakenham have been described and published by Mr Jim Baldwin and colleagues in the Fakenham Local History Society. Consequently, a detailed account of the schools of the town and the town's printing industry will not be documented here. It is the aim of this book to complement these existing publications and to present a comprehensive account of the development of the town and its surrounding region.

E.M. Bridges

Chapter 1. Development of the Landscape

This account will begin with an introduction to the development of the landscape of North Norfolk and the site of Fakenham. There are two distinct phases in the geological history of the area, the formation of the very old underlying 'solid' rocks and the much more recent accumulation of large masses of unconsolidated sands and gravels referred to as 'drift'. It is the latter which provides the diverse landscape of the Fakenham area, proving that all of Norfolk is not, as Noel Coward stated, 'very flat'. The geology of the Fakenham area was first mapped by Woodward (1884), a more recent appraisal of Norfolk geology has been written by Funnell and Pearson (1984). (A summary of the local geology may be found in Bridges (2003).

The Solid Geology
To trace the development of the landscape of North Norfolk we must first understand the underlying geology upon which everything else rests. It is convenient to begin the story at Hunstanton where the rocks forming the foundation of Norfolk may be seen in the cliffs (Fig. 1.1)

Fig. 1.1 The Cliffs at Hunstanton (Photo: E.M.Bridges)

During the Cretaceous period of geological time, between 146 and 65 million years ago, this part of the British Isles was submerged below the sea where sediments accumulated. The lowest bed visible is an iron-rich sandstone, called Carstone which is succeeded by the Hunstanton Red Rock (equivalent to the Gault Clay of S.E. England). At the top of the cliff is the Chalk which was laid down in the waters of a warm sea which extended widely throughout Europe. There was prolific marine life present, including marine algae. These algae had, as part of their structure, tiny calcareous plates, called coccoliths assembled into spheres, composed entirely of calcium carbonate which, when they died fell to the sea bed and accumulated to form the pure limestone called chalk (Toghill, 2005)(Fig. 1.2).

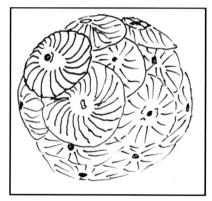

Fig. 1.2 A coccolith x 8000

Altogether as much as 500m of chalk accumulated in Norfolk. As it accumulated, the chalk included many layers of flint nodules, reputed to have formed from spines of siliceous sea urchins and sponges, but more plausibly from silica weathered from the land and brought down rivers to the sea where it was precipitated and subsequently turned into flint.

At the beginning of the Tertiary period there was an increase in movement of parts of the earth's crust. America began to drift away from Europe and there was an increase in volcanic activity. Many species of animal became extinct, among them the ammonites and the last of the dinosaurs. At this time also, a large asteroid collision with Earth left a widespread thin layer of iridium, and the subsequent devastation may have reduced food supplies dramatically causing these extinctions.

In the early phase of the Tertiary, sandy and gravelly sediments accumulated over the Chalk in the subsiding North Sea basin, and later the London Clay accumulated as the waters became deeper.

However all this came to an end with the great mountain-building episode when the Alps were thrust up as Africa collided with southern Europe. The outward ripples of this continental convulsion also raised much of Britain above the sea. The rocks below Norfolk were given a gentle eastwards slope, reflected in the underlying structure of the Chalk (Fig. 1.3). Towards the foot of the dip slope the sandy and gravelly Tertiary beds remain in the eastern part of the county.

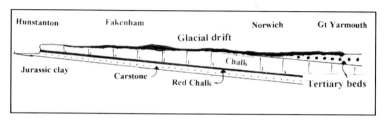

Fig. 1.3 Geological section, Hunstanton to Gt. Yarmouth

When the map of 'solid' geology is consulted (Fig. 1.4), it presents a very simple appearance with the Chalk escarpment in the west, extending southwards from Hunstanton with a wide dipslope exposing successively younger strata of chalk forming a plateau extending eastwards as far as Norwich where it passes beneath the Crag sands and gravels. The upper surface of the Chalk is taken by the eastward dip to 500 ft below sea level at Yarmouth.

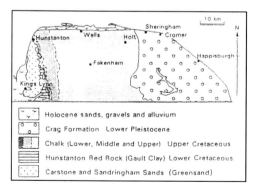

Fig. 1.4 The Solid geology of North Norfolk

3

The Drift Geology

Although the solid geology forms the basis of the landscape, it does not take a professional geologist to appreciate that there are few outcrops of Chalk across Norfolk. It is well and truly covered with a great mixture of unconsolidated rock materials which in places are many metres thick (Fig.1.5). This material, called glacial drift or till, results from the activity of continental ice sheets during the Pleistocene period which lasted some two million years, including the last half a million years of earth history when East Anglia was affected by at least three successive advances of the ice which accumulated over Scotland and Scandinavia. These colder periods were interspersed by warmer interglacial periods.

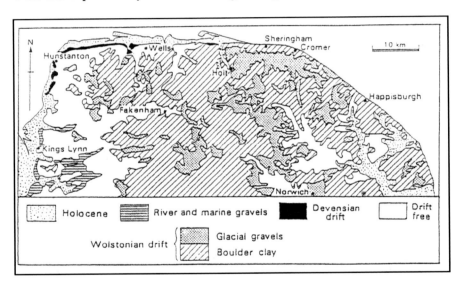

Fig. 1.5 Drift geology of North Norfolk

The oldest of these glaciations, 300,000 years ago, is called the Anglian Glaciation (Fig. 1.6). As the ice melted it left behind masses of rock debris which it had scraped off the land over which it flowed. Erratic pebbles from Scotland and Scandinavia are frequently found, so it must be assumed the ice originated from those areas. A re-advance of this ice pushed forward crumpling the deposits known as the Cromer tills into a feature with contorted beds called a 'push

4

moraine' which forms the Cromer Ridge (Banham and Ransom, 1965; Bristow and Cox, 1973). To the south of the Cromer Ridge the drainage system of the river Bure developed .

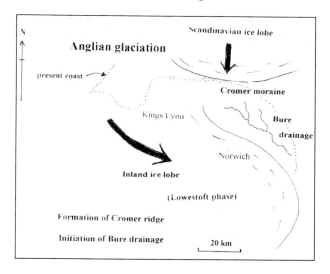

Fig. 1.6 The Anglian glaciation (300,000 to 250,000 years ago)

After a warmer interglacial phase (Hoxnian), from which some of the earliest human artefacts have been found, a second glacial phase followed called the Wolstonian glaciation around 130,000 to 200,000 years ago (Fig. 1.7). This also approached Norfolk from a northerly direction but in so doing brought with it large amounts of Jurassic clays and ground-up chalk which it scraped-off the outcrops in Lincolnshire and west Norfolk. This chalky boulder clay, or marl, is widespread in north and northwest Norfolk (Straw, 1960). The ice which brought this deposit did not over-run the Cromer Ridge, but swept around it, extending as far south as Cambridge. Other ice streams from the Midlands caused the removal of as much as 30m of the Jurassic clays from the Fenland basin and extended as far south as the river Thames. The ice pushed almost as far as London and caused the diversion of the river Thames from a course across mid-Essex towards the centre of the North Sea basin to its present course.

5

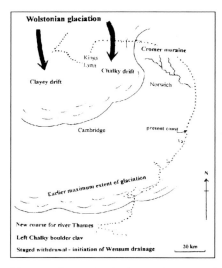

Fig. 1.7 The Wolstonian glaciation (200,000 to 130,000 years ago)

In the succeeding warmer period, called the Ipswichian, melting of this icecap resulted in the establishment of the course of the river Wensum.

The last glaciation to impinge upon Norfolk again approached from the north but reached its limit on the North Norfolk coast, with a lobe of ice pushing through the Wash gap between Hun-stanton and Boston to further erode the Fenland basin (Fig. 1.8). Called the Devensian glaciation, the maximum extent of this icecap occurred between 25,000 and 13,000 years ago (Straw, 1979: Suggate and West, 1959).

Fig. 1.8 The Devensian glaciation (25,000 to 13,000 years ago.)

Although the Fakenham area was not directly affected by this episode, the ice mass reached the Norfolk coast and the Fakenham area endured a periglacial environment in which the unconsolidated drift deposits were smoothed by downhill

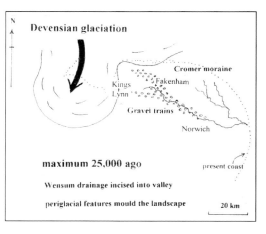

sludging and the now dry valleys upstream of the present Wensum headwaters were developed. Gravels which had weathered out of the earlier drifts were subject to cryoturbation (frost churning) in the cold tundra-like climate.

With large amounts of water locked in the continental-size ice

6

cap, sea levels were lower, allowing the rivers to lower their beds, cutting down through the unconsolidated deposits to the underlying chalk. The large amounts of flood water from the seasonal melting of the ice formed gravel spreads, some of which remain preserved on the interfluves (Fig.1.9).

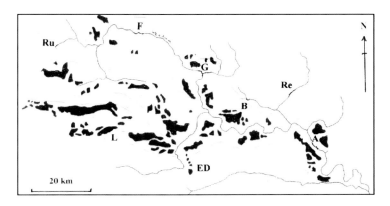

Fig. 1.9 Gravels spread by glacial melt water
F = Fakenham, Ru = Rudham, G = Guist, Re = Reepham, B = Bawdeswell,
L = Litcham, ED = East Dereham, A = Attlebridge

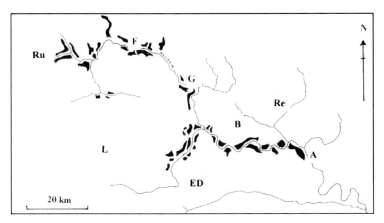

Fig. 1.10 In-valley terraces of the River Wensum
F = Fakenham, Ru = Rudham, G = Guist, Re = Reepham, B = Bawdeswell,
L = Litcham, ED = East Dereham, A = Attlebridge

Subsequently, within the river valleys as a result of the process of meandering and down-cutting, sandy river terraces were left on the valley sides (Fig.1.10). It is upon one of these terraces that Anglo-Saxon invaders decided to make a settlement which became Fakenham.

The growth of peat in the valley in post-glacial time, both upstream and downstream of Fakenham made crossing the Wensum valley difficult, forcing people to use sites where the sandy river terraces constricted the width of the valley floor. The most significant of these constrictions was between Fakenham and Hempton. Throughout late Neolithic, Bronze Age and Iron Age times, increasingly the land was being cleared and cropped for short periods until soil exhaustion set in. The light sandy surface soils of the Fakenham area underwent soil erosion and eroded soil material was washed into the river valley overlying the peat deposits. Excavations prior to the construction of the Tesco supermarket in Fakenham revealed 2 to 3m of peat overlying chalk in the valley bottom. Above the peat is a blue-grey fine sandy or silty alluvium to a depth of 2m.

The site of Fakenham

The explanation for the site of Fakenham may be seen most clearly in the cross section of the valley side near Fakenham Library (Fig. 1.11). Three separate levels may be discerned: the lowest at 35m above sea level is the flood plain of the river Wensum upon which

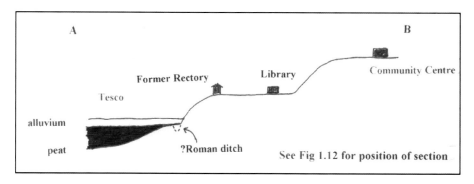

Fig. 1.11 The site of Fakenham

the Tesco supermarket has been built. At 40m above sea level is Oak

8

Street, this is the almost level terrace feature upon which Fakenham is sited; it extends northwards to Wells Road and southwards into the Market place and swings eastwards along Norwich Street and Norwich Road. Finally, at 45m above sea level is the spur of higher land upon which are built the Community Centre and the Church which overlooks the Market Square.

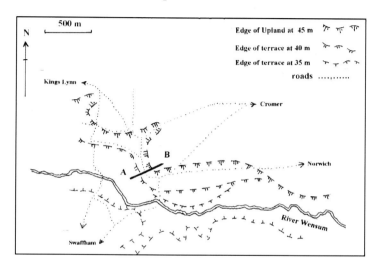

Figure 1. 12

The relationship between the local topography and the road pattern is shown on Figure 1.12. Wells Road can be seen to descend from the higher ground onto the terrace feature near the Sixth-Form College and the roads leading towards Holt and Norwich both rise as they leave town. South of the market place, terraces on both sides of the river are only a short distance apart making a convenient valley crossing point linking Fakenham and Hempton.

The final phase of the geological history of the Fakenham area continues to the present day as the river carries its load of fine soil particles in suspension and other substances in solution. Some of the sediment is temporarily laid down on the river floodplain, but in the long term it will be taken up again on its way to the sea.

The valleys of the Glaven, Stiffkey and Burn

Whilst Norfolk is generally thought to be lacking in relief, the area immediately north of Fakenham has some fairly abrupt relief associated with the valleys of the small rivers which drain directly to the North Sea.

A study of outwash plains in the Glaven valley suggests glacial melt waters flowing away from the glacier front through a gap in the Cromer ridge at Briston to join the river Bure (Straw, 1973). At the time when these fluvial features were deposited further west, the ice margin extended in a lobe further south, possibly almost reaching Fakenham. Within this area, a line of gravels known as Blakeney Downs has been interpreted as a deposit of gravels by water flowing within the ice cap called an esker (Grey, 1997). If this is correct, then this transitory lobe of ice which extended into North Norfolk probably left an arcuate depression on retreating, scoured by melt water which has become the route of the Stiffkey river through East Barsham.

Further complications occur in the lower reaches of the valley at Stiffkey where the small stream enters a broad meander before reaching the sea. This section of the valley has all the hallmarks of a glacial overflow channel which was probably linked to others along the north coast of Norfolk which accommodated melt waters from the Devensian phase of glaciation (Bridges, 1998). By contrast the valley of the Burn appears to have a simpler origin, rising at Leicester Square Farm and flowing through North and South Creake and Burnham Thorpe to reach the sea at Burnham Overy Staithe.

Geological postscript

Earthquakes in Norfolk are neither frequent nor severe but an earth tremor (Richter scale 5.2) occurred on 27th February, 2008 which shook Fakenham. Little damage was reported to domestic property, but the reredos behind the high altar in the Parish Church was badly cracked and separated from its wall fastenings. It was repaired in 2009.

References

Banham, P.H. & Ranson, 1965. 'Structural study of the contorted drift and disturbed chalk at Weybourne, North Norfolk.' Geological Magazine 102: 164-174.

Bridges, E.M. 1998. Classic Landforms of the North Norfolk Coast. Geographical Association, Sheffield.

Bridges, E.M. 2003. Geology and Scenery in the Fakenham District. Fakenham Museum.

Bristow C.R. and Cox, F.C. 1973. 'The Gipping till: a reappraisal of East Anglian glacial stratigraphy.' Journal of the Geological Society of London 129:1-37.

Funnell, B.M. and Pearson, I., 1984. 'A guide to the Holocene geology of North Norfolk.' Bulletin of the Geological Society of Norfolk 34:123-140

Grey, J.M. 1997. 'The origins of the Blakeney esker, Norfolk.' Proceedings of the Geologists Association 108: 177-182.

Larwood, G.P. & Funnell, B.M. eds 1961. 'The Geology of Norfolk.' Bulletin of the Geological Society of Norfolk. Special (edition).

Straw, A. 1960. 'The limit of the 'last' glaciation in North Norfolk.' Proceedings of the Geologists Association 71: 379-390.

Straw, A. 1979. 'Eastern England.' In: Geomorphology of the British Isles: Eastern and Central England. pp 1-139. Methuen.

Suggate R.P. & West, R.G. 1959. 'On the extent of the last glaciation in Eastern England.' Proceedings of the Royal Society of London, Series B. 150: 263-283.

Toghill, P. 2005. The Geology of Britain. Airlife Publishing, Crowood Press, Malmsbury.

Woodward, H.B. 1884. Geology of the country around Fakenham, Wells and Holt. Memoir of the geological Survey of Great Britain.

Chapter 2. The River Wensum

The area drained by the River Wensum is 593 square kilometres. Its tributaries are the River Tat, Langor drain, Guist drain, River Tud, Blackwater, Swannington beck, Penny Spot beck and Wendling beck (Fig. 2.1) (Sear, et al., 2006). Fakenham is the largest settlement sited on the banks of the River Wensum.

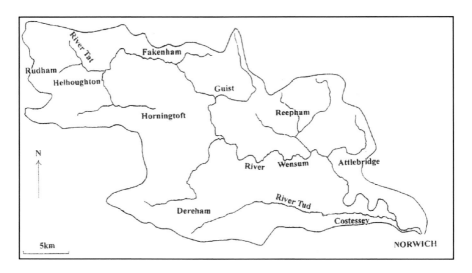

Fig. 2.1. Catchment of the River Wensum

According to the Ordnance Survey, (1:63360 Seventh Series, revised 1950) the River Wensum has its source at West Rudham, and three miles downstream it is joined by the River Tat rising on Syderstone Common. There is some controversy over the source of the river as its longest headwater rises near Horningtoft, then flows through Raynham Park, draining the area south and south-west of Fakenham. Some people claim that this tributary is the real source of the River Wensum. These small tributaries come together to form the Wensum a mile north of the village of Helhoughton. The river then flows in a generally south-easterly direction past Fakenham to Norwich. The springs which source the river Wensum are from the chalk aquifer and lie between 50 and 60m above sea level. The river has a steady fall throughout its length until it reaches tidal conditions after joining the Yare in Norwich.

The Wensum is described scientifically as a groundwater or base flow stream; 85% of its flow comes from groundwater originating from the underlying Chalk aquifer as springs (Environment Agency, 2000). The remaining 15% is derived from surface run-off and direct recharge. As a result the Wensum is not normally liable to severe flooding; it is not a 'flashy' river. However, floods have occurred in 1912 (Baldwin and van Damme, n.d.) and in the 1940s, but since then the river channel has been modified to lessen the liability of flooding. The river's flow regime generally rises and falls seasonally, peaking in March and April as a result of autumnal rains which have percolated through the overlying sands and gravels to the chalk beneath. Exceptionally heavy summer rainstorms or winter rainfall combined with melting snow may result in flooding. Former gravel extraction ponds may help to damp down high flows and they also provide surfaces for evaporation. Falling from 60m above sea level to its tidal junction with the river Yare, the Wensum has a gradient of 1 in 1400 (Fig. 2.2).

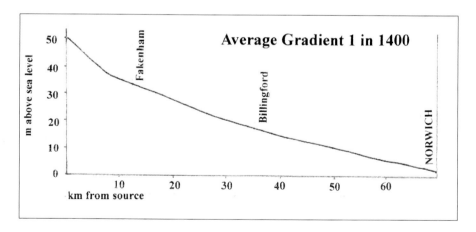

Fig. 2.2. Gradient of the River Wensum

Gauging stations are located at Fakenham, Swanton Morley and Costessey which monitor the variation of flow throughout the year. Figures from the Fakenham gauging station indicate that the mean flow in 2003-2004 was 4.3m³ per second. The maximum flow was 15m³ per second and the minimum flow 1.1m³ per second. The annual march of the river's regime can be seen in figure 2.3. Water flowing in a river transports soil material to the sea. This sediment

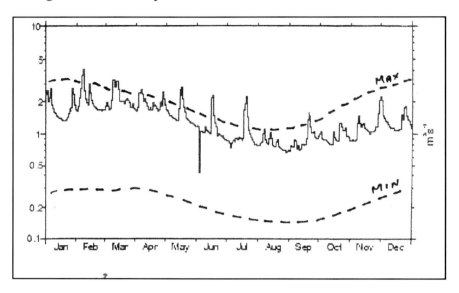

Fig 2.3. Maximum and minimum daily mean flows 1967-2001.
(Trace is for 2001)

originates from the channel bed, channel banks and land surface adjacent to the river and land drains. Sediment is moved by two mechanisms: suspended sediment transport in which clay, silt and fine sand are carried suspended in the water and as bed load transport in which sand creeps along the bed of the river (gravel remains stationary as normal flows are insufficient to move it). The total sediment load in 2003-2004 was calculated to be 1,994.2 tonnes.

Throughout the medieval and modern period up until a few years ago, the power of running water was a valuable asset for a community. However with the Wensum, the low gradient of the river forced modifications on its course to increase the flow to drive water-wheels. For example at Sculthorpe and Fakenham the river was diverted to one side of the valley from its original course (in both cases this can be seen by the course of the parish boundary). In this way a fall of about 1m was obtained to drive the mill wheel.

Since the Middle Ages fourteen mills are known to have been constructed on the River Wensum which have modified the flow and course of the river in different ways. Upstream of a mill the water was impounded causing still water and sedimentation. Downstream of a mill, where the water flow is faster, the river bed was scoured to its gravel bed. In order to provide the mills with sufficient water, the river was widened for storage purposes. Since the mill at Fakenham ceased to be used, the width of the river has been reduced to encourage a faster flow of water.

None of the mills are now operative, but the sluices remain and the buildings have been modified into apartments. In order from the source, the list of extant mill sites includes Sculthorpe, Fakenham, Ryburgh, Billingford, Elsing, Lyng, Lenwade, Taverham and Costessey mills. There is evidence also of a mill at Shereford and a Malt mill was sited near where the railway crossed the river at Fakenham (Malt Mill Common). Hempton mill, known as Goggs mill, fell into disrepair before the First World War and was finally demolished shortly after the Second World War, to be replaced by a bridge.

Pollution in the Wensum valley
Improved sewage treatment in the past few decades has reduced greatly the potential for pollution by raw sewage. There are 28 sewage works, which efficiently remove unwanted material from the waste water which still contains enhanced levels of phosphorus when discharged into the river. Siltation from farm drains has increased over the past 30 years; it decreases light penetration into the water and brings nitrogen and pesticide residues from the fields. There is some eutrophication of the river leading to prolific weed growth, but insufficient to deplete the water of oxygen. In this respect, the presence of several mill sluices helps to maintain a healthy oxygen content as the water falls through the mill sluices and into the mill pool. There are 12 industrial plants including gravel works, a maltings and food processing plants within the catchment. Drainage from roadsides contains oil and petrol and salt in winter.

References

Baldwin, J. and van Damme, n.d. Another Look at Fakenham. Jim Baldwin Publishing, Fakenham.

Environment Agency, 2000. Conservation Strategy for the River Wensum.

Sear, D.A. et al. 2006. Geomorphological Appraisal of the River Wensum Special Area of Conservation. Report 685 English Nature.

Chapter 3. Soils and Ecology in the Fakenham district

As Norfolk is an important agricultural county, there has been a significant interest in its soils over the past three centuries. In the 18th century, Marshall (1787) and Kent (1796) commented on the soils in their general appraisals of the agriculture of the county. Young (1804) for the Board of Agriculture, and Trimmer (1846) from a geological point of view, also described in general terms the soils of the county. Woodward (1902) discussed the soils and subsoils of Norfolk and Newman (1912) and Nicholson and Hanley (1935) gave accounts of soils and agriculture and soil conditions in East Anglia respectively. Raynes (1935) and Perrin (1961) gave accounts of Norfolk soils for meetings of the British Association for the Advancement of Science.

In the immediate vicinity of Fakenham, the Soil Survey of England and Wales has compiled a detailed soil map on the 1:25,000 Ordnance Sheet TF82 (Helhoughton) (Corbett, 1897); other detailed surveys have taken place around Sheringham (Sheets TG13 and TG14), Harleston (Sheet TG28), north-west of Norwich (Sheet TG11), in the Bure valley (Sheet TG31), and in the Waveney valley (Sheets TG28 and TG49). The broad picture of Norfolk soils is given in the Soil Survey's 1:100,000 Soils of Norfolk and the 1:250,000 map and bulletin Soils and their Use in Eastern England (Hodge et al., 1984).

The pattern of soil over the landscape is complex as the nature of any soil is dependent upon several factors including the underlying geological parent material, its position on the landscape, the vegetation growing (or that has grown) upon the site, the hydrological conditions as well as the influence of human beings. During the process of mapping soils, profiles were described in detail from districts where they commonly occurred. Thus, the Newport series, a brown earth formed in glacio-fluvial sands was first mapped and described near Newport in Shropshire. A peat soil first described in the Fens is called the Adventurers series. The locally described Fakenham series has a slightly stony, fine-loamy topsoil overlying a clayey, brightly coloured B horizon attributed to previous weathering in a past (inter-glacial) climatic period.

Soils are distinguished from one another by their profile, the appearance of the soil in section from the surface to the underlying geological material, otherwise known as the parent material (Fig.3.1). A soil profile consists of a number of layers, called horizons, which result from the activity of the soil-forming processes. In simple soils there are three horizons often referred to by the letters A, B and C which are distinguished by differences in colour, structure and texture. Some soils with a more complicated history have additional horizons developed such as are associated with leaching, these are indicated by E. Subsidiary characters present in horizons are indicated by lower case letters such as: plough horizon (p), unploughed humus horizon (h), weathered material (w), increased clay content (t), and saturation by water (g).

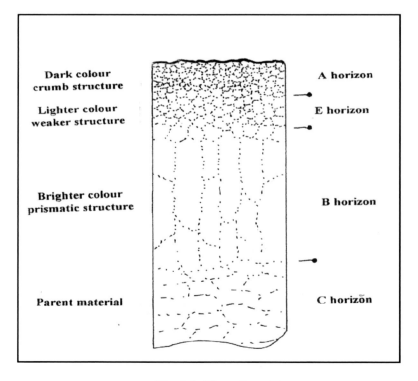

Fig. 3.1. The soil profile

The A horizon is enriched with organic matter which in cultivated soils is the topsoil. It has a wide variety of living organisms present which are responsible for the conversion of fresh organic matter into humus and its incorporation into the soil. The B horizon has different colours, structure, texture and moisture conditions from horizons above or below. Because it is less subject to alteration by human activity, the nature of the B horizon is frequently used in the classification of soil for scientific purposes. In some sandy soils, the B horizon is merely leached and weathered to acquire a rusty brown colour; this is a Bw horizon. In other soils the B horizon has received clay washed down from the overlying A horizon, markedly increasing its clay content, this is a Bt horizon. Slow draining conditions will give the B horizon a mottled appearance or in extreme cases a dull grey colour, called a Bg horizon.

The C horizon is the material from which the soil has been formed i.e. its parent material. This parent material may be a solid rock such as a limestone, sandstone or shale, or in East Anglia is more likely to be the highly variable rock debris left behind by the glaciations of the Pleistocene some 300,000 years ago and again 250,000 years ago. As the ice-cap melted the rock debris which the ice had scraped off the land surface was dumped in an unsorted mass ranging from a few centimetres to tens of metres thick.

After it was deposited, the older drift material was subject to weathering between the major glacial episodes as well as further weathering in the current episode of soil formation. The B horizon of many local soils has preserved evidence of soil formation which dates from between the two last major glacial episodes. It consists of an increased clay content and has a coarse blocky or prismatic structure and because of slow drainage has become weakly mottled by reduction of iron compounds. Because of this previous history of soil formation, many local soils are known as 'palaeo-argillic earths'.

In the final phase of glaciation, when ice only impinged on the North Norfolk coast, a periglacial climate (tundra conditions) prevailed and blown sand was added to the soil surface. Also, the soil material was subject to down slope mass-movement (solifluction) which smoothed the landscape and exposed older drift deposits on the shoulders of hills. The Fakenham soil series occurs where these older, already weathered, deposits have been revealed.

Lastly, as a result of Neolithic clearance and cultivation, large areas of North Norfolk became very acid heathland which was lightly grazed. In the medieval period, only the village's open fields

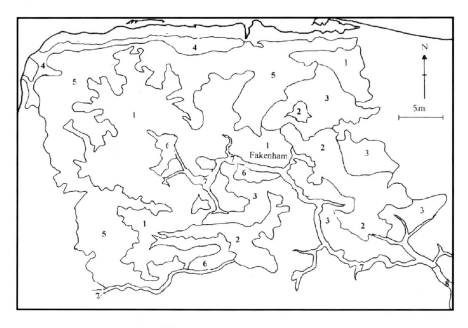

Fig.3.2 Simplified soil map of the Fakenham district.
Key to associations: 1. Barrow, 2. Beccles, 3. Burlingham, 4. Hunstanton, 5. Newmarket, 6. Newport, 7. Isleham, 8. Adventurers

(After 1:250,000 Soil Survey of England and Wales map of Soil of Eastern England).

would have been cultivated regularly and received manure, but even so their fertility declined. In the 18th century the pioneers of the agricultural revolution enclosed the land and developed the technology to manage these soils and to make this area around Fakenham one of the most productive agricultural areas of England.

Local soils

In order to make a map of soil distribution it is necessary to classify soils within a mapping unit composed of soils with similar characteristics. Detailed soil maps, at 1: 25,000 or larger scales may have individual soil series or even phases depicted, but smaller scale maps bring similar soil series together in inclusive groupings called soil associations. These associations are in turn included within the major soil groups of the world.

The major soil groups present in the catchment of the upper Wensum valley contain associations of the sandy or gravelly, freely drained Brown Soils, or the slowly draining Stagnogley Soils with clayey subsoils on upland areas. Alluvial Gley Soils, Earthy peat soils and peats are found on the Wensum flood plain where they are influenced by groundwater (Fig 3.2). Detailed information on these associations of soils may be obtained from the publications listed in the references. However, one local soil grouping is worthy of comment as it bears the name Fakenham series.

The Fakenham Series

The Fakenham Series is classified by the Soil Survey of England and Wales as a typical palaeo-argillic brown earth and is a member of the Barrow association. This soil has a fine-loamy texture overlying clayey chalky drift. The Fakenham Series has its B horizon formed in material weathered between the two major glacial episodes that took place in the district. Erosion on the shoulder of hills has brought this inter-glacially weathered material near to the land surface and this has later been covered by a thin mantle of blown sand which now forms the A horizon (Fig.3.3). The B horizon has hues of 7.5YR or redder and has coarse mottles suggestive of slower drainage. The parent material, lying below the B horizon, is the chalky boulder clay which consists of a ground-up mixture of clay and chalk fragments of the chalky drift deposited in the Wolstonian phase of glaciation. It is this material, marl, that was exploited for soil improvement in the agricultural revolution, leaving a large pit in almost every field. In so doing, the 19th century landlords changed this area from acidic heathland into a fertile agricultural region. The profile description is as follows.

The Fakenham Series profile

Ap	0 - 27 cms	Greyish brown (10YR5/3) slightly flinty sandy clay loam. Fine sub angular blocky structure in surface 10 cm. Moderate to coarse sub-angular blocky in lower part of horizon, porous, dry, weak ped strength, few roots, slightlycalcareous, smooth boundary.
2Bt	27 - 53 cms	Strong brown (7.5YR 5/6) weakly mottled with 5/6) weakly mottled with yellowish brown (10YR 5/6). Slightly flinty clay. Large blocky or prismatic structure with many clay coatings, firm ped strength moist, non calcareous, few fine fibrous roots sharp wavy boundary.
Cu	53 - 90 cms	Mottled light brownish grey (2.5Y 8/2) and yellowish brown (10YR 5/6) slightly flinty and chalky clay, moist, massive structure, firm ped strength, very calcareous, abrupt boundary.
2Cu	90+ cms	Extremely chalky glacial till.

Notes

Description follows the style and definitions of the Soil Survey of England and Wales handbook for soil description.

Colours are defined by the Munsell Soil Colour Chart.

Subscripts of main horizon designations denote ploughing (p), increased clay content (t) and unspecified character (u).

As has been demonstrated in the Helhoughton area, a distinct pattern of soils may be seen in the landscape which includes the Fakenham soil series. The distribution is closely related to a soils position on slopes resulting from the action of soil forming processes acting both vertically and down-slope.

The Importance of Soils

Soils are a major support system of human life and welfare as they largely determine the productive capacity of the land. Soils provide the greater part of food for humans and animals through the crops

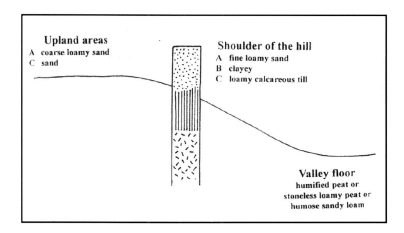

Fig.3.3. Position of the Fakenham series in relation to relief

grown and natural vegetation. They are major determinants of natural terrestrial ecosystems or biomes; they are sources, transformers and stores of plant nutrients; they form a nearly endless mosaic of small 'reactors' on the land surface where plant and animal residues are re-cycled.

Soils are buffers and filters for pollutants and are important sources and sinks in biogeochemical cycles involving carbon dioxide, methane and nitrous oxides, gases known to produce global warming. Soils are a key buffer system in the world's hydrological cycle, absorbing water and smoothing flood peaks.

Successful agriculture and security of food supplies rely upon the sustained and successful management of soils. An adequate level of organic matter in topsoils is necessary for maintenance of soil structure which helps soil stability. Careful cultivation to avoid erosion also is essential; each 100 tonnes of soil lost per hectare represents a total loss of 2,000-2,500kg of humus, 2-300kg of nitrogen, 1-200kg of phosphate and between 500 and 1000kg of potash. If fertility is to be maintained, these nutrients must be replaced and this is not possible by organic means alone. As will be seen in a later chapter, 18th century landowners in the Fakenham district were the first to learn how to manage their soils and greatly increase productivity.

Ecology

It is perhaps understandable that biologists have tended to concentrate their studies upon those areas with semi-natural vegetation such as the Breckland heaths, the wetlands surrounding the Broads or the coastal marshes to the exclusion of the agricultural areas. In spite of this neglect, there is a wealth of different habitats that co-exist with agricultural activity. The majority of the land area around Fakenham is devoted to arable agriculture, but despite the intensive nature of this predominant land use, there are many miles of hedgerows and many small woods which encourage wildlife. To some extent this is because the large estates fostered hunting and shooting and so maintained areas of woodland and covert for the game birds.

However, in the immediate area of Fakenham the River Wensum and its riparian zone is the focus for considerable conservation activities. Most of the Wensum catchment (393ha) is designated a Site of Special Scientific Interest (SSSI). It contains over 100 species of plants and 23 species of fish and also includes areas of adjacent fen, reed beds and wet grassland (Baker et al, 1978). The riparian zone provides a range of habitats and this is reflected by the presence of nature reserves at Sculthorpe Fen, run by the Hawk and Owl Trust, at Hempton Common run by the Norfolk Ornithological Trust and the Pensthorpe reserve which hosted the BBC's Springwatch programme in 2008 and 2009.

Flora

The floodplain has a number of significant habitats including grazed meadows, reed beds, fen, marsh and riverside trees. The upper reaches of the River Wensum may be divided into those with a gravel bed and those with a silty bed. Where gravel bed prevails, the lesser water-parsnip and brook water-crowfoot grow, but where there is a silty or muddy bed, spiked water milfoil, blue water-speedwell, opposite-leaved pondweed, willow moss and the rare short-leaved starwort may be found.

In the middle and lower reaches of the Wensum, the bed is predominantly of a silty nature and yellow water-lily, flowering rush, fennel pondweed, perfoliate pondweed, arrowhead and unbranched bur-reed occur. Also present are rigid hornwort, fan-leaved water-crowfoot, horned pondweed and common club-rush.

Fauna

The aquatic fauna of the River Wensum includes molluscs, mayflies, caddis flies, stone flies, water beetles and whirligig beetles. There are white-clawed crayfish, Demoulin's snail, and flatworms. Twenty species of fish occur, with brown trout the most common and dace, eels, brook lamprey, with bullhead, chub, pike and roach more common in lower reaches.

Avian fauna associated with the river valley include duck, grebes, kingfisher, heron, reed warbler, gadwall, pochard, grey wagtail, marsh harrier, barn owl, snipe, lapwing and oystercatcher.

In addition to the human occupants of the valley, the mammalian fauna include rabbits, rats, otter, water vole, five species of bat, muntjac and roe deer.

References

Baker, R., Driscoll, R.J. & Lambley, P. 1978. 'The River Wensum'. Norfolk & Norwich Naturalists Society 24;(4) 197-219.

Corbett, W.M. 1987. Soils in Norfolk VII Sheet TF82 (Helhoughton). Soil Survey Record No.106. Harpenden.

Hodge, C.A.H., Burton, R.G.O., Corbett, W.M., Evans, R. and Seale R.S. 1984. Soils and their Use in Eastern England. Harpenden.

Kent, N. 1776. General View of the Agriculture of Norfolk.

Marshall, W. 1787. The Rural Economy of Norfolk.

Newman, L. F. 1812 Soils and Agriculture of Norfolk. Nicholson H.H. & Hanley, F. 1935. 'Soil Conditions in East Anglia'. Empire Journal of Experimental Agriculture 3. 60-74.

Raynes, F., 1935. The Agriculture of Norfolk, British Association for the Advancement of Science, Norwich.

Trimmer, J. 1846. On the geology of Norfolk as illustrating the laws of distribution of soils. Journal of the Royal Agricultural Society 7. 444-485.

Woodward, H.B. 1902. 'The soils and sub-soils of Norfolk.' Transactions of the Norfolk and Norwich Naturalists Society 7. 421 - 485.

Young, A. 1804. General View of the Agriculture of Norfolk. Board of Agriculture.

Chapter 4. Human colonisation of the Fakenham area

Stone Age colonisation
Evidence for occupation in the Fakenham area by people during the Palaeolithic (Old Stone Age) and Mesolithic (Middle Stone Age) is rare, but stone hand axes dating to pre-glacial times (700,000 years ago) have been found at sites on the coast of Norfolk (Figs. 4.1 & 4.2). However, as glaciation has intervened their provenance is not certain. A very worn quartzite hand axe has been found at Stibbard (Wymer, 2005), but it too could have been moved by glacial activity. No other signs of habitation by these people have been found.

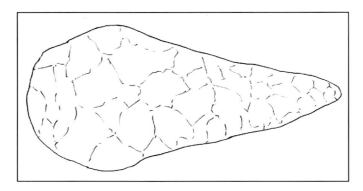

Fig. 4.1 Palaeolithic hand axe

The tribes of Homo sapiens who came from Africa into Europe were nomadic hunter-gatherers who spread northwards and westward from the Middle East region. It has been suggested that the loss of dark skin pigment in Europeans was related to the need for vitamin D as those with lighter skins adjusted better to the lower intensity of the sun in northern climates. It is certain that they hunted near the periphery of the ice-cap during the last advance of the ice in the Devensian, some 25,000 years ago. On the steppes of Ukraine they even constructed dwellings using mammoth bones. At the time of this last glacial maximum, sea level was much lower and

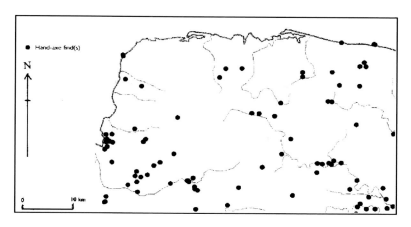

Fig. 4.2 Palaeolithic hand axe finds in the Fakenham district
From Map 7, Ashwin T.M. & Davidson A.J. (2005) Artefact distribution data.
© Norfolk Museums & Archaeology Service

passage on foot was possible across what is now the bed of the North Sea from mainland Europe. With the retreat of the ice margin around 10,000 BP (Before Present), scattered evidence has come to light that these early humans were present in Norfolk, such as in the lower Wensum valley, at Titchwell and on Kelling Heath, but they left no evidence in the immediate Fakenham area. As the climate ameliorated, the vegetation would have gradually colonised the former tundra, changing it from a treeless plain to coniferous forest and eventually to deciduous forest. Animal species would have followed, taking advantage of the forest extension. The Mesolithic hunter-gatherers possibly may have managed these forests for game, but their environmental impact was minimal.

Neolithic settlers

With the arrival of the Neolithic people came the beginnings of cultivation. The origins of farming practice occurred in the Middle East, but there is no consensus why the change from hunter-gathering to settled agriculture took place. By the nature of their lives, foragers must be nomadic, moving on when fresh food supplies are required. Farming implies sedentary occupation of the land, accumulating stores of food for winter and seed corn for the following year.

It is a commonly held idea that when Neolithic people came to Norfolk they tended to favour lightly wooded terrain, rather than the densely forested areas. Finds of Neolithic axes, dating from 6000 BP are common in the area west of Fakenham between the Rudhams and the river Nar, and sites where flints were mined occur also. These were not on the scale of Grimes Graves.(Fig. 4.3)

Fig 4.3 Pit No. 1 Grimes Graves (Photo E.M.Bridges)

At this period burials took place in long barrows, two of which are at West Rudham. A clue to the possible stability of Neolithic society is the spread of pottery, which after 4500 BP became highly decorated and this period of human history is often referred to as that of the 'Beaker Folk'. Food gathering almost certainly continued to take place throughout the Neolithic period, but increasing use was made of settled agriculture for food supplies. The soils of North Norfolk have a sandy topsoil and were lightly wooded and the assumption is made that such lands would have been easy to clear and cultivate. However, light soils have the disadvantage that they hold little moisture, have a low content of plant nutrients and once cleared soon lose what little fertility they have through cropping or leaching by rain. Erosion of cleared land would also have been a problem. Elsewhere in Norfolk a radiocarbon-dated pollen sequence indicates that extensive clearance took place from 1700 BP, later aided by the use of bronze tools.

A late Neolithic henge was first noticed from the air in 1929 at Arminghall south-east of Norwich and investigated in 1935. It consisted of a circular ditch 27m in diameter within which was a

Fig. 4.4. Seahenge
(Photo © N. Hoffman, Thornage Hall)

horse-shoe-shaped construction, revealed by the presence of post holes. Its opening faced a gap in the ditch system. Recently, the discovery of a henge at Holme has caused much interest (Fig. 4.4). This interesting feature was revealed in 1998 after erosion by the sea had removed a covering of sediment on the foreshore. It consisted of a circle of upright wooden posts in the centre of which was an inverted tree trunk. The structure has been dated to 4050 BP. Considerable controversy surrounded the removal of the wooden henge from the seashore and its preservation and installation in a

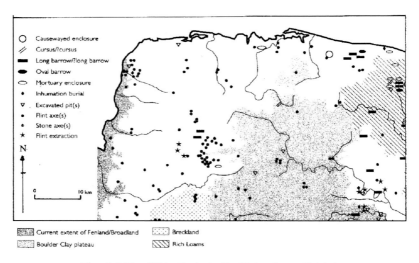

Fig. 4.5 Neolithic finds in the Fakenham district
From Map 9, Ashwin T.M. & Davison A.J. (2005) Artefact distribution data.
© Norfolk Museums & Archaeology Service

museum at King's Lynn.(Champion 2000) However, if it had been left in situ it would have been eroded by the sea or suffered depredation by trophy hunters. Preservation means that this 4000 year old structure will be available to be seen by future generations. Numerous finds of artefacts of this period suggest that the area around Fakenham must have had a moderate density of population as the area is surrounded by burial mounds with particular clusters near Houghton, at Weasenham and Pensthorpe (Fig. 4.5). An arrow-head dating back to 3800 BP was found on Fakenham Heath and a polished flint axe-head of Neolithic or Bronze Age was found in Fakenham cemetery; one or two other finds of this period have been made but their provenance is uncertain.

Bronze Age
Introduction and adoption of agriculture removed the necessity for daily food-gathering and enabled the society of the day to support non-productive members including metal-workers, priests and chieftains. Evidence of Bronze Age occupancy is widely and evenly spread, with finds occurring on both sandy and clayey soils in Norfolk. There is still a lack of evidence of permanent settlements,

30

but the spread of artefacts might suggest that a semi-nomadic lifestyle continued into the Iron Age (Fig. 4.6). After about 2700 BP, Hutcheson and Ashman (2005) suggest that people lived in small groups in unenclosed villages or hamlets and that their

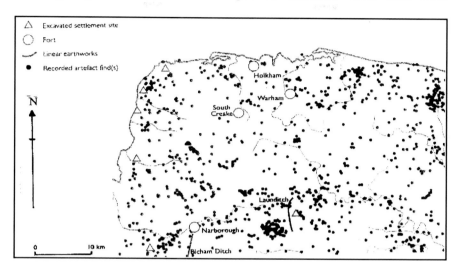

Fig. 4.6 Iron Age finds in the Fakenham district
From Map 11, Ashwin T.M. & Davison A.J. (2005) Artefact distribution data.
© Norfolk Museums & Archaeology Service

lifestyle continued into the Iron Age (Fig. 4.6). After about 2700 BP, Hutcheson and Ashman (2005) suggest that people lived in small groups in unenclosed villages or hamlets and that their migration probably took place gradually as buildings were constructed on new plots rather than on previous sites of habitation. However, there is little factual knowledge of how their society was organised.

Iron Age
In terms of human advancement, iron tools were an improvement on bronze ones and the Iron Age period saw also the development of 'Celtic' art forms and coinage. Iron Age earthworks, particularly in western Norfolk, have survived. Possibly these were tribal centres or secure places into which people retreated when danger threatened. At Warham is situated the best example of a circular

31

Iron Age earthwork with double banks and ditches (Fig. 4.7) with an adjacent rectangular enclosure in the next field. A similar circular enclosure at Bloodgate Hill, Creake, has been ploughed out, but geophysical survey has revealed a single earthwork and ditch, a central ring enclosure and areas segregated by linear features. Another example occurs at Holkham, partly protected by saltmarsh, but little is known about it.

Fig. 4.7. Warham Camp
Photo © E.M.Bridges

In 1980 crop marks near Thetford indicated the presence of an archaeological structure. It turned out to be a first century AD rectangular ditched enclosure containing nine fences surrounding five circular buildings. Dubbed Boudicca's palace, it was clearly a place of some significance with speculation that it might have been an artificial grove of religious significance (Wade-Martins, 2000).

Some evidence of early trackways has persisted in the landscape to the present day. The Icknield Way possibly dates back as far as 8000 BC and in the immediate Fakenham area, the road known as Norwich Long Lane (now partly under the bypass) is thought to be a pre-Roman trackway (Robinson and Rose, 2008).

References

Ashwin, T. and Davison, A. 2005. An Historic Atlas of Norfolk. 3rd Edition. Phillimore, Chichester.

Bahn, P.G., 2002. The Atlas of World Archaeology. Greenwich Editions, London.

Bond, R, Penn, K and Rogerson, A. 1990, Norfolk Origins 2 The North Folk; Angles, Saxons and Danes. Poppyland Publishing, Cromer.

Briers, F. (Ed), 1961. Norwich and its Region. British Association for the Advancement of Science, Norwich.

Champion, M. 2000. Seahenge: a Contemporary Chronicle. Barnwell, Aylsham.

Clarke, R.R. Archaeology. In Norwich and its Region. B.A.A.S., Norwich.

Hutchinson, N and Ashwin T 2005, in: Ashwin, T. and Davison, A. 2005. An Historic Atlas of Norfolk. 3rd Edition. Phillimore.

Robinson, B. and Rose, E.J. 2008. Roads and Tracks Norfolk Origins 2 Poppyland Publishing, Cromer.

Robinson, B. and Gregory, T., 1987. Norfolk Origins 3 Celtic Fire and Roman Rule. Poppyland Publishing, Cromer.

Topping, P. 2003. Grimes Graves. English Heritage, London.

Wade-Martins, P., 2000. Discovering our past. In: Norfolk Century: the People and Events. Ed. T. Heaton, Eastern Counties Newspapers.

Wymer, J., 'Late Glacial and Mesolithic Hunters (c10,000-1000BC)' In: Ashwin, T. and Davison, A. 2005. An Historic Atlas of Norfolk. 3rd Edition. Phillimore.

Chapter 5. Fakenham Emerges

The preceding account has few specific references to Fakenham although it is fairly certain human beings were living in the area and exploiting its natural resources. These people were Celts of the Iceni tribe and they have left only a small imprint on the Norfolk landscape. The etymology of a few place names is virtually the only evidence of their occupation of the land. The names of the River Ouse and Lynn both have Celtic derivations as do the names of the villages of Trunch and North and South Creake.

The Romans first reconnoitred Britain in 55 BC and subsequently, under the command of Julius Caesar, invaded in 54 BC, penetrating as far as St Albans before withdrawing. In 43 AD, in the reign of Claudius, a full scale invasion took place. At first the Romans had an agreement for the Iceni in northern East Anglia to rule themselves as a 'client' kingdom, but following the death of King Prasutagus and the suppression of the revolt by his widow, Boudicca, in 60/61AD, the land of the north folk was taken fully into the Roman empire. Roads were constructed linking towns and forts on the coast as at Brancaster (Branodunum). The Icknield Way was an ancient track along the foot of the chalk escarpment, and may have been improved by the Romans. They utilised the Peddars way and another road was constructed through Kempstone and Toftrees to the coast. This road bypassed the site of Fakenham in the vicinity of Sculthorpe mill leading towards the coast and now forms the western boundary of Holkham Park (Fig. 5.1). Neither the Peddars Way nor this road led directly to the Brancaster fort. Near Wighton, several buildings and a fort of Roman age have been identified east of Copy's Green and in the Great Walsingham area evidence has come to light of a settlement at which metal-working and pottery-making took place. From Toftrees another road headed eastwards through a settlement at Billingford to Brampton. Roman coins were found in 1869 during building work on Queen's Road in Fakenham which were probably hidden by their owner about 340-370 AD. A ditch of Roman age was discovered in Oak Street when a dig took place to reveal Fakenham's medieval rectory (see Fig.6.14).

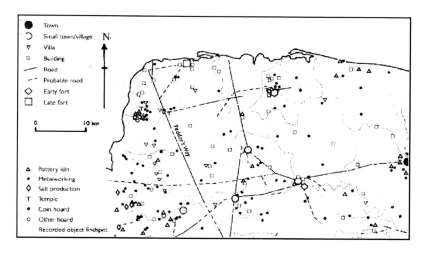

Fig. 5.1 Evidence of the Romans in the Fakenham area
From Map 13, Ashwin T.M. & Davidson A.J. (2005) Artefact distribution data.
© Norfolk Museums & Archaeology Service

The Romans withdrew in 410 AD leaving the locals to defend themselves against the Anglo-Saxons and later the Danes. There had been raids in the 4th century during the Roman occupation that developed into a migration of Anglo-Saxon people from Northern Germany in the 5th century. Subsequently, raiders and settlers came from Denmark in the 9th century (Bond et al., 1990). Evidence from cemeteries of the Anglo-Saxon period indicate a complete break with preceding Celtic traditions, grave goods recovered being almost entirely of a Germanic nature. At this time bodies were cremated and the ashes placed in an urn and buried with their belongings, rather than beneath a tumulus.

Significant evidence of the Anglo-Saxon invasions can be deduced from place names (Fig. 5.2). The suffix 'ham' is common throughout Norfolk and it is thought to have been given to earlier settlements: 'ham' refers to 'the lands of' a particular person: 'tun' was given to a farm or small secondary settlement. Both are combined with a personal name to give the place name. Places ending in 'ham' frequently occur on freely drained sites near river valleys whereas those with 'tun' occur in a more widespread distribution. In the case of Fakenham, we may imagine an Anglo-

Saxon adventurer, Facca, coming up the river Wensum and claiming the site of Fakenham for his lands. An alternative explanation of the name Fakenham is given in Blomefield's Norfolk as 'the river on which this town stands, might, in the Saxon age be called Fa; ken always denotes a stream of water or river' and ham refers to the land as described previously. By the time of the Domesday survey the spelling had become Fachenham.

When our adventurer Facca landed, what did he find? The river would have flowed at a slightly lower level on its alluvial plain and above the alluvium would have been a level terrace-like feature which would have caught his eye as a potential site for his settlement. Away from the immediate foreground he would have seen a landscape over which the semi-nomadic Celtic people had migrated. Their actions had reduced large areas on sandy soils to heath. Some areas elsewhere, as in Breckland, had even become areas of mobile sand dunes.

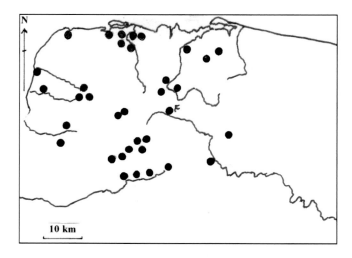

Fig.5.2 Anglo-Saxon place names with the element ham.

Fakenham developed into a settlement, probably of a few 'tofts' along a trackway which we now know as Oak street, the Market place and Norwich street, with a branch track leading down to the ford across the river to Hempton. Using evidence from neighbouring 'lost' villages, the possible early distribution of tofts in Fakenham is shown in Fig. 9.2. Some stonework attributed to the Saxon period is incorporated into the present church walls. Sadly there is little other visual evidence of early Saxon occupation of the site of Fakenham.

However, at Spong Hill near Elmham, a cemetery with more than 2000 cremation pots and 58 graves was in use from the 5th to the 8th centuries (Penn, 2005). Anglo-Saxon cemeteries have been recorded at ninety places in Norfolk and the one at Spong Hill has been most thoroughly investigated. Two thousand three hundred cremation urns dating from 450 to 600 AD were found, the grave goods revealing fascinating sociological links between these settlers and their former Germanic homelands. The settlement nearby had huts and post-built houses. Other cemeteries occur in the headwaters of the Wensum and in the Walsingham area. A Saxon grave was discovered in 1869 at a site near Norwich Long Lane, Fakenham, which contained a bronze brooch, buckles and strap ends, dating from the 6th or 7th century AD.

Elmham has been claimed in the past to be the site of a Saxon Cathedral. This designation arises from a 1950s excavation when the ruins were identified as a 'Cathedral' (Rigold, 1960). The remains of several wooden structures, presumably earlier versions of the cathedral, were found on the site. There was indeed the seat of a Saxon bishop from 680 AD until 1071 when the seat was removed to Thetford. After the new church was built the cathedral was converted to a fortified manor house or a chapel for the use of the bishop. The village houses and cemetery extended into Elmham Park on the other side of the present road, and the foundations of a large timber building there may have been the manor house.

It has long been thought that ton settlements were of a secondary phase of occupation, but current thinking suggests that this may not necessarily be true in all cases - they may simply be subsidiary settlements, often given a directional name e.g. north, south, east, west, or the name comes from the practice of growing particular crops e.g. Appleton (apples) or Barton (barley). Referring briefly back to the Celtic period in the context of place names, most locations in Norfolk were given new names by the Romans and the Anglo-Saxons, leaving very few Celtic names for posterity (Fig. 5.3).

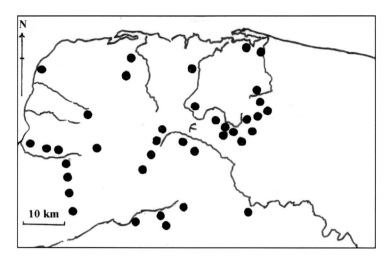

Fig. 5.3 Anglo-Saxon place names with the element *'ton'*

Anglo-Saxon names suggestive of woodland have caught the imagination of archaeologists who have sought to envisage the geography of past times. It might be expected that the finer-textured soils of central Norfolk would have retained woodland as these would have been most difficult to clear and cultivate with Iron Age equipment, but this is not necessarily borne out. South of Fakenham is a cluster of names ending in 'ley' which suggests clearance of woodland for pasture. On the light-textured soils of the Cromer area, the name Holt means wood. Names with the element lea (meadow), breac (clearing) and feld (open country) imply open land, but perhaps only in comparison with adjacent wooded areas. Immediately south of Fakenham, Toftrees is derived from toft (house or home) and hris (woodland). The central area of Norfolk still contained the greatest extent of woodland at the time of the Domesday survey.

The final wave mainland invaders coming to settle in Norfolk were from Denmark and Scandinavia (Fig. 5.4). There is a major concentration of 'Viking' names in Flegg, north of Yarmouth, where many settlements have the place name ending by, but elsewhere a probable later phase of invaders led to settlements in the vicinity of Fakenham using the place name element thorpe such as Sculthorpe, Thorpland and Pensthorpe. Finds of metallic objects of Scan-dinavian design are widely but thinly scattered throughout North and West Norfolk. Weights and brooches have been found in the valleys of the Burn, Stiffkey and Glaven as well as in the vicinity of Sculthorpe and Colkirk near Fakenham.

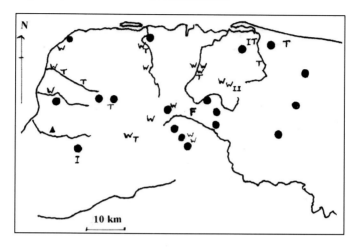

Fig. 5.4 Evidence of Scandinavian settlement in the Fakenham area.
● - place name elements   T – brooches   W – weights I - ingots

References
Ashwin, T. and Davison, A.   2005. An Historic Atlas of Norfolk. 3rd Edition. Phillimore
Bond R., Penn K. & Rogerson A., 1990 Norfolk Origins 4 The North Folk: Angles Saxons & Danes. Poppyland Publishing, Cromer
Bridges, E.M. 2005. Lost Villages in the Fakenham District. Fakenham Museum.
Bridges, E.M. 2005. Place Names in the Fakenham District. Fakenham Museum.
Darby, H.C. 1951. An Historical Geography of England Before AD 1800, CUP
Ekwall, E. 1936. Oxford Dictionary of English Place Names. OUP
Penn, K. 2005. 'Early Saxon Settlement'. In: Ashwin, T. and Davison, A. 2005. An Historic Atlas of Norfolk. 3rd Edition. Phillimore
Rigold, S.E. 1960. North Elmham Saxon Cathedral. Ministry of Works, HMSO.
Robinson, B. and Gregory, T. 1987. Norfolk Origins 3 Celtic Fire and Roman Rule. Poppyland Publishing, Cromer.
Rye, J. 1991. A Popular Guide to Norfolk Place Names. Larks Press.
Schram, O.K. 'Place Names' In: Norwich and its Region. BAAS, Norwich
Wade-Martins, S. 1984. A History of Norfolk. Phillimore, Chichester.

Chapter 6. Medieval Period of Fakenham's History

By the time of the Norman Conquest of England in 1066, a settled rural pattern of existence was well and truly established in the Fakenham area. The manorial system governed the way of life and provided a stable if unequal society. At last, the story of Fakenham enters the period of history when written records survive, including the Anglo-Saxon Chronicle and the Domesday Book. It cannot have been an idyllic period, because as soon as the protective arm of the Romans was withdrawn, raiding first by Anglo-Saxons and later by Vikings increased, and eventually settlement took place. Some settlers may have been mercenaries brought in to help defend the east coast during the Roman occupation. Many artefacts of the pre-Norman period have been found in East Anglia, most notably at Sutton Hoo in Suffolk, which provide a guide to life at that time.

Arguably, one of the most important events in British History was the 1066 invasion of the country by William of Normandy. Following the defeat of King Harold at the Battle of Hastings, the Conqueror took possession of the whole land and divided it between his tenants-in-chief. Where resistance was encountered the Normans laid waste significant areas of land. It is suggested that some idea of the depredations can be inferred from the differences in figures for 'waste' between 1066 and 1086 (Darby, 1951). The towns were not immune either, as 22 burgesses of Norwich fled to Beccles and those who remained were ruined through forfeiture of their possessions, fines and taxes levied by King William.

Domesday Fakenham

The survey commissioned by William the Conqueror and recorded in the Domesday Book gives a valuable picture of the country at the time of the Norman conquest in 1066, and at the time of its compilation 1086. Fakenham had several outliers (beruites) in Alethorp, Thorpland, Stanhoe, Stibbard, Creake, Barsham, Kettlestone and Pudding Norton. In translation (Brown, 1984), the entry for Fakenham is as follows:

> The hundred of GALLOW. In Fakenham Harold held 2 ploughs.

of land before 1066. Always 5 villagers; 20 smallholders; 4 slaves.

Always in lordship 2 ploughs; 4 men's ploughs; woodland for 12 pigs; meadow, 5 acres; 3 mills; half salt-house. Always 3 cobs; 20 pigs; 200 sheep

To this manor belong

1 outlier, Alethorpe at 1 c. of land.

Always 3 smallholders; 1 slave.

In lordship 1 plough; the men; meadow, 2 acres.

Also another outlier, Thorpland, at 1 c. of land. 1 plough; 1 slave.

Further, 1 outlier at 2 c. of land in Creake.

Always 10 villagers. Then 11 smallholders, now 4.

Always 1 plough in lordship. Then 3 men's ploughs.

Now meadow, 1.5 acres. Always 1 cob; 30 pigs; 80 sheep.

Also 4 freemen at 6 acres; 1 plough.

Another outlier, Stanhoe, at 1 c. of land.

Always 3 villages

Then 1 plough in lordship, now 2 men's (ploughs).

In Stibbard 3 free men.

Also in Barsham 1 (?free man) and in (Little) Snoring 3 free men;

among these free men 3 acres of land. Always 1 plough.

Value of all this before 1066 £8; now £43. Fakenham has 7 furlongs in length and half in width, 12d in tax. Stibbard has 3 furlongs in length and 2 in width, 12d in tax.

In (Pudding) Norton a church, 8 acres; (value) 6d.

Hempton was also in Gallow Hundred; its entry was as follows:

> In Hempton 4 free men, at half c. land. 4 smallholders; 1 plough.
> 1 church, at 1 acre.
> value then 5s; now 3s.

Fakenham, being a small place, probably did not attract too much attention in these turbulent times, but it is on record that the Manor of Fakenham, which had belonged to King Harold, was given by King William to Earl de Warrene, whose family held it until 1377 when it passed to the Duchy of Lancaster, so acquiring the town's full name of Fakenham Lancaster. Interpreting the Domesday record, it is thought between 100 and 150 people lived in Fakenham at that time. The common fields were situated to the north of the town as is commemorated by the road names Field Lane and Highfield Road, and as partially indicated on maps which pre-date the Ordnance Survey. The fields were sub-divided into areas in which individual people farmed strips, scattered throughout the common fields. The strips were marked by grass edges or low baulks. An indication of the possible extent of Fakenham's open fields is given by a map of the location of the glebe lands which formerly belonged to the church. Many of these plots of land are shown in strip form, scattered across the area known to have been Fakenham Fields (Fig. 6.1)

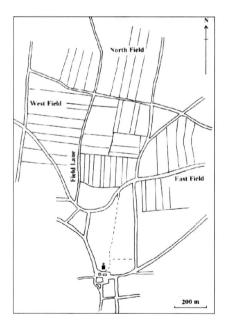

Fig. 6.1. Possible common fields of Fakenham

It was the practice to crop in strict succession each of the fields in the following manner. After a fallow year during which cultivations kept weeds to a minimum, wheat or rye was sown in the autumn and harvested in the following August; the stubble would be grazed by cattle or sheep which provided manure and after ploughing in spring, barley or oats sown for harvesting in August. After grazing, the land again went back into fallow. Designed to extend the fertility as much as possible, the cropping and natural leaching of plant nutrients left the common fields on a downward spiral of fertility which could not be sustained indefinitely.

In the 'fold course' system which was practised in the Fakenham area, the Lord of the Manor had the right to graze sheep on the commoners' arable strips after harvest and until sowing next year. Sheep were grazed on the heath and common lands during summer, but after the hay was cut they grazed meadows in the Lammas shack. They also grazed the stubble after the wheat, barley or oat crops were taken in the Michaelmas shack. These practices were evolved by common consent but disintegrated in late medieval times when the price of wool increased and rapacious landlords rode roughshod over established customs (Yaxley, 1995). Small farmers found that the excessive numbers of sheep made it nearly impossible to farm their arable strips as they had done in the past and were forced to leave their cottages.

Rural medieval life was largely governed by the 'Rights in Common' which were enjoyed (allowed) by the villagers (Hoskins, 1958). It has been mentioned that grazing could take place on the common arable fields after harvest, but the Rights of Common refer particularly to grazing on commons, in woodland and waste. In effect, these rights allow a tenant farmer to take a profit from the land owned by the lord of the manor. For some villagers these rights made the difference between life and death by starvation in many years. The rights were:

Pasture:	the right to pasture animals
Pannage:	the right to let pigs forage, especially in woods
Turbary:	the right to dig turves (peat)
Estovers:	the right to take wood from common land for fuel or agricultural implements
Piscary:	the right to take fish from particular waters
Right in soil:	the right to take stones from the surface

There appears to have been little woodland in the Manor of Fakenham, but reeds, furze and small timber could have been gathered from the commons. Common grazings were also an integral part of medieval agriculture. Those of Fakenham were mainly on the Wensum valley floor (Figs. 6.2, 6.3, 6.4) and on heathland which extended around the eastern side of the settlement (Fig. 6.5). In the adjacent settlement of Hempton, common grazings occurred on the valley floor, but also on the larger Hempton Green (Fig. 6.6).

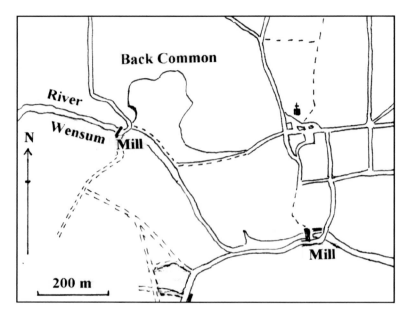

Fig.6.2. Back Common, Fakenham

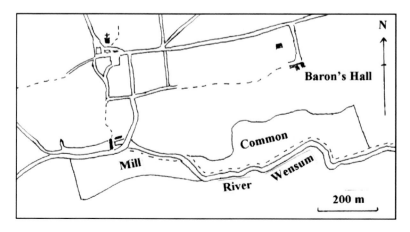

Fig. 6.3. Mill Common

44

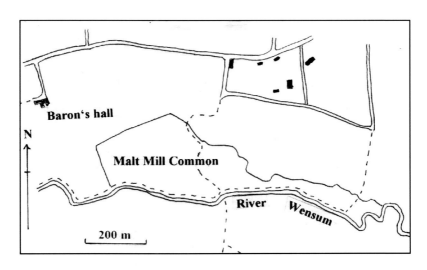

Fig.6.4. Malt Mill Common, Fakenham

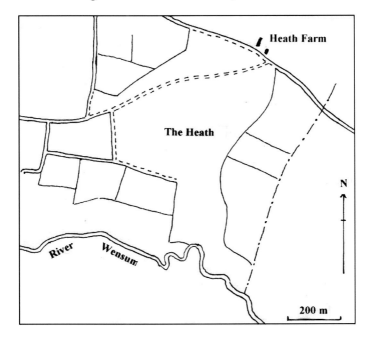

Fig. 6.5. Fakenham Heath

Hempton Priory

After the Norman Conquest, in the reign of Henry 1 (1068-1135), the Hospital of St Stephen was founded by Roger St Martin and Richard West (Nicholson, 1977). The hospital was a place where hospitality was given to pilgrims and travellers, but it was eventually converted into a priory with three or four Austin canons of the Order of St Augustine. These canons were unlike the other great monastic orders in that they had no central organisation and were simply a group of people who lived a communal life of worship.

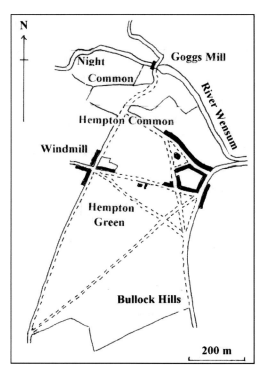

Fig.6. 6. Hempton Commons and Green

Some had taken holy orders and served nearby churches as parish priests. Hempton Priory comes into the medieval picture of Fakenham as its Prior was responsible for the upkeep of the causeway between Hempton and Fakenham. Inevitably this led to friction, especially as the townsfolk of Fakenham wanted pilgrims travelling to Walsingham to pass through the town, rather than pass by on the western side. In these disputes, Fakenham is referred to as the Manor of Fakenhamdam and the priory as Damnesende as it was situated at the southern end of the causeway or dam.

A further controversy took place in 1297 when the Lord of the Manor of Fakenham objected to the Prior of Hempton using pastures in Pudding Norton. In the following year a charge was brought against the Prior that he was taking goods from land at Waterden to Creake Fair. The priory actually owned land at

Waterden, but nevertheless the Prior was imprisoned and the goods expropriated, so it appears some sharp practice was taking place on one side or the other. A list of the Priors of Hempton is given by Blomefield.

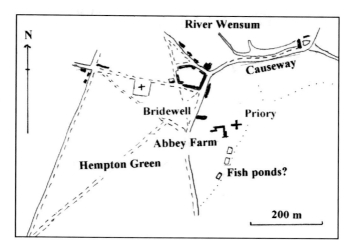

Fig. 6.7 Site of Hempton Priory and Bridewell

Hempton Priory appeared on a list of monasteries to be suppressed in 1536. The King's Commissioners duly appeared and a rather pathetic inventory of the Priory's goods was made (Fitzjohn, 1956). Dissolution of the Priory left Hempton without a church or clergyman as the original Hempton Church on Shereford Road had been allowed to become ruinous. A 1552 inventory of church goods at St Stephen's suggests that they struggled on, but a final date of closure is not known. Other small Austin houses were located at Coxford 8 km west of Fakenham and at North Creake.

Larger, more significant institutions were founded in Walsingham by the Augustinian (c.1153) and Franciscan orders. Walsingham later became an important site for pilgrimage following the vision of Richeldis which told her to build a 'holy house' in the grounds of the Abbey. Binham Priory, a Benedictine foundation, dates from 1093, and Castle Acre, where the first Cluniac priory was built by William de Warenne, from 1087. (Wade-Martins, 1984).

Medieval weaving trade

Only two professional weavers are recorded in probate records for Fakenham and the town was situated at the extreme western edge of the area where most Norfolk weaving took place (Evans, 2005). As with weavers in Snoring and Little Walsingham they were not involved in the worsted trade. A law in 1337 gave protection to the early immigrants from the Low Countries who brought with them their weaving skills. Known as 'Strangers' they helped to make the area rich as can be seen in the magnificent churches which occur throughout the area north and north-west of Norwich. A further influx of textile workers in 1567 brought Dutch and Flemish skills into Norwich itself. In 1771, Arthur Young estimated that there were 12,000 looms and 72,000 people involved in the weaving trade in Norfolk.

The numbers declined in the 18th century as the industry became mechanised and moved to Yorkshire where water power was more plentiful and later coal supplies for steam engines to drive the looms was more easily available.

The Black Death 1348-9

A steady growth of population took place until 1349 when the Black Death reached Fakenham. Simultaneously, a period of adverse climate was accompanied by poor harvests and consequent starvation. Large numbers of the weakened population throughout Britain succumbed to the disease, but figures for Fakenham are not available. It may even have escaped the impact of the disease elsewhere. Until recent times the many abandoned villages in the Fakenham area were thought to be the result of plague. However, recent research into the history of these villages indicated that many were abandoned long after the time of the plague (Cushion et al. 1982).

Peasants Revolt 1381

After the Black Death (1348-9) there were fewer peasants to work the land and the prospects for work and pay were greatly enhanced for the survivors. However, most villagers were tied to the land and legally bound to their masters. Strict enforcement of these regulations for labour and collection of dues fomented dissatisfaction and eventually led to riot and the death of their leader, Wat Tyler. A dyer from Felmingham, named Litster, probably a minor landowner in his own right, led a rebellion in 1381. They marched on Norwich and camped on Mousehold Heath. Nuns at Carrow were forced to hand over deeds (containing legal contracts for labour) which were burnt and the castle was besieged. The rule of authority was restored by Bishop Despenser who made the revolutionaries retreat to near North Walsham where they were defeated. Litster was beheaded and quartered, the four pieces of his body being sent to Norwich, Lynn, Yarmouth and his home village. A monument stands beside the Norwich to North Walsham road. Nobody is recorded taking part from Fakenham, but Great Walsingham, Binham and Houghton St Giles people were involved (Cornford & Reid, 2005).

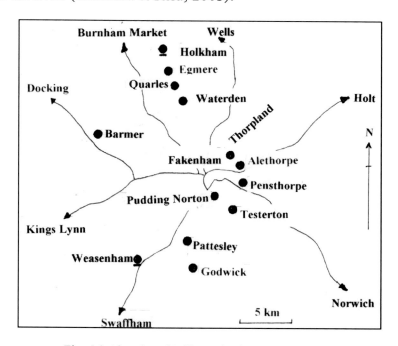

Fig. 6.8 Abandoned Villages in the Fakenham area
● - abandoned   ● village moved

49

Abandoned villages

In the district surrounding Fakenham there are several villages which were abandoned, during the medieval period. Other villages were moved in the process of emparking (Holkham, Houghton and West Raynham) or simply moved (Weasenham) (Fig. 6.8). The most common sign of an abandoned village is a ruined church or tower as at Godwick, Pudding Norton or Egmere, situated in a pasture field with many humps and hollows which make it difficult to plough. From the air, the pattern of individual plots of land, 'tofts' surrounded by banks and ditches, and the linear features of sunken roadways (hollow-ways) passing through the village, can be seen. Some examples follow (Cushion et al, 1982).

Until the 15th Century, Godwick was a small village, which suddenly declined to less than 10 households in 1428, almost 100 years after the Black Death. A survey of 1508 recorded 11 empty properties out of 18 on the north side of the village street. The village had a mill and a church, dating to Norman times, the tower of which still stands, although it has been partially re-built (Fig. 6.9). In the days before the Coke family moved to Holkham, Edmund Coke built a manor house (now demolished) on part of the village. The abandoned village may be visited and notice boards describe what to look for on the site. In this case it is probable that inclement summer weather and a succession of poor harvests on clayey, slow-draining soils could have caused its demise. By 1595 the village had gone and only the ruins of the church remained.

Thorpland, like Fakenham, belonged to King Harold at the time of the Norman Conquest, but by 1316 had been included in the parish of Fakenham and in 1334 was not even listed. Thorpland had it own chapel dedicated to St Thomas and in 1496 there were 26 tenants. In 1520 the tenants brought a case against Henry Fermor of East Barsham Hall (a London merchant who had married well). He had ruthlessly acquired land, and enclosed it for sheep grazings, but he also pastured sheep on the open fields and common land, making farming uneconomic for the small tenants. The church had become a barn by 1611 and now only a fragment remains in the private gardens of Thorpland Hall. A similar story may be told of Alethorpe and Pensthorpe where sheep again dominated the use of the land at the expense of the tenants.

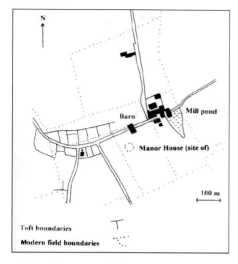

Fig. 6.9 Plan of Godwick
(from Cushion et al. 1982)

The church at Alethorpe became a barn in 1602 and a fragment only of the Pensthorpe church may be seen in the wall of the restaurant at the Nature Reserve.

At Pudding Norton, the aerial photograph clearly shows the ruined church, the tofts and the road passing though the village site. Altogether there were 22 tofts and the church of St Margaret which dates from the 12th Century (Fig. 6.10). The Domesday survey recorded 60 acres, a bordar, half a ploughland and half an acre of meadow, 7 sokemen (freemen but with obligations to the manor) who had 20 acres and one plough team.

Fig. 6.10 Plan of Pudding Norton.
(from Cushion et al 1982)

Documentary evidence suggests a population of 70 in 1329 and there was no reduction of taxes paid after the Black Death, which suggests the village escaped the plague. The Fermor family again was probably to blame for pasturing sheep as a son of the man at Barsham appears to have owned the village. The church had become a ruin by 1602.

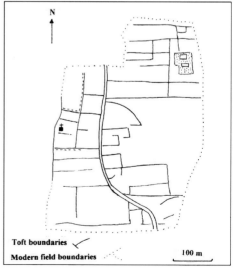

Kett's Rebellion 1549

Enclosure of commons and other grievances against the gentry led to civil unrest in many parts of Norfolk and in Hethersett fences were knocked down by villagers who, under the leadership of Robert Kett, a tanner, marched to Norwich in protest. They camped on Mousehold Heath and recruited more and more supporters until their numbers reached around 16,000. They were told to disperse but refused. Then they proceeded to storm Bishopgate, entered the City and took the mayor and other people prisoner. A small force under the direction of the Marquis of Northampton failed to quell the riot and again they refused to disperse. Reinforcements in the name of the Earl of Warwick arrived on 23rd August and again asked them to disperse, but this was ignored. A battle took place at Dussindale where 3000 were killed. Kett was caught, taken to London, charged, convicted and brought back to Norwich to be hanged. No supporters of the rebellion have been recorded from Fakenham, but rebels are identified from East Barsham, Great Ryburgh and The Burnhams (Rutledge, 2005).

Medieval Markets

Documentary evidence of markets in villages and towns exists, most records dating back to the 1200s. However, many of these markets were known to be abandoned by the 17th century (Dymond, 2005). A few survived by virtue of their nodal position where people could gather together for trade and exchange of goods. In the Fakenham district, Burnham Market had one of the oldest markets, dating back to 1209, Walsingham's market can be traced back to 1226 and Fakenham's to 1286. However, it is certain that places of barter and exchange pre-dated these earliest market records.

Many villages around Fakenham also are recorded as having markets in the early medieval period. Hempton, Great Ryburgh, The Creakes, Docking, Pensthorpe, Helhoughton, North Elmham and Wells but many of these were no longer in use in the 17th century. It is noticeable that after the Black Death, very few new charters for markets were granted. Hempton is an interesting case as it retained three large fairs, two for cattle on Whit Tuesday and 22nd November and one for sheep on the first Wednesday in September. Permission to hold a fair on Hempton Green was granted by King John in 1200.

By the 17th century cattle were being driven from Scotland by drovers to the cattle fair in November where they were bought and fattened by local farmers before being driven on to Smithfield market in London. Bullock Hills on Hempton Green is said to be where the cattle were kept during these cattle fairs. Horses also were sold during the November fair. A small sheep fair was held each year from the 13th century but in 1848 an outbreak of disease occurred at Harpley fair and Hempton was used as an alternative site, making it the most significant sheep fair in the county. Hempton sheep fair prospered throughout the 19th century and continued until 1969 when the last sheep were sold by this method.

After the Civil War

Except for King's Lynn, Norfolk was chiefly dominated by gentry on the Parliamentary side in the Civil War, and no significant battles were fought in the county. Cromwell is reputed to have spent a night at Fakenham in a barn in Oak Street, and a cottage in Tunn Street is named after him. Fakenham passed through this period of political upheaval without harm, but the citizens had to pay taxes for the maintenance of the Parliamentary Army as documents of 1646 and 1649, authorised by Rice Gwynn, Robin Sheringham and Will Sheldrake, show. Rice Gwynn was a distinguished lawyer of the Inner Temple who purchased a manor in Fakenham in the early 1600s. He subsequently became a JP and was recorder of Norwich and Yarmouth. He was never accepted by his neighbours whom he described as 'unrulie and evill-disposed people not regarding [him] or anie thinge [he] did or could do for them.' Gwynn died in 1630 and memorials to the family may be seen in the parish church.

Of great significance for the town was the arrival in Fakenham after the Civil War of Edmund Peckover. When he was discharged from Cromwell's army, Peckover set up as a merchant in 1657, and members of the family remained in Fakenham until 1836. The first bank in town was founded by Peckover, eventually linking with the Buxtons, Gurneys and Birkbecks, who had banking interests elsewhere, and finally becoming Barclays. This dynamic family of Quakers had an important impact upon the business and religious life in Fakenham. As well as occupying a house on the Market Place, following the Act of Toleration in 1689, they also built a Meeting

House in Quaker Lane (a block of flats now stands on the site) and their cemetery is the small enclosure with trees on Old Lane opposite the Aldiss Superstore. Edmund Peckover had three sons: Joseph stayed in Fakenham, Edmund went to Bradford where he was a banker and wool chandler, and Jonathan, who went to Cambridge-shire where he was a banker, eventually became the Lord Lieutenant of that county. A museum in Wisbech commemorates his achievements.

Daniel Defoe travelled through Norfolk in 1723 and gives a momentary glimpse of life in the county. He commends the 'diligence spread over the whole country' and the 'vast manufactures' of the weaving and spinning cottage industries. Speaking of eastern Norfolk which he describes as 'very populous and throng'd with great and spacious market towns', he includes 'East Deerham' and several other market towns. The countryside is said to be 'exceeding fruitful and fertile, as well in corn as in pastures'. He mentions cattle being brought from Scotland by drovers for sale at St Faith's for fattening. After visiting Yarmouth and Cromer, he heads round the coast to Wells commenting on the trade with Holland from the small ports of the Norfolk coast and the dangers to shipping. The shrine at Walsingham is commented on as are the 'seats of the two allied families of Lord Viscount Townshend and Lord Walpole', but his route takes him on to King's Lynn, and he makes no mention of Fakenham.

Fakenham's archaeological dig

A mandatory archaeological dig took place on an Oak Street site before the construction of the Tesco supermarket in 2004-5 (Wessex Archaeology 2003, 2006). It was known that a medieval rectory stood on the lower part of the land which in later times became part of the agricultural engineering works of Southgates and more recently Edmondsons. The earliest surviving map of Fakenham, which is dated 1650, shows a building surrounded by a rectangular moat with the words 'The scite of the Rectory' inscribed on the plot of land (Fig. 6. 11). One side of the moat survived until the middle years of the 20th century as is confirmed by its presence on the 1948 1:25,000 Ordnance Survey map.

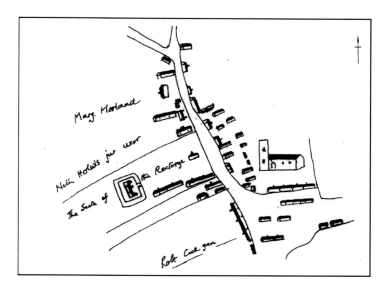

Fig. 6.11. Rectory site shown on the 1650 map.

The moat surrounding the rectory was not constructed for defensive purposes, rather it was for reasons of contemporary fashion. This medieval rectory is thought to have been abandoned by 1677, but the Georgian rectory was not built until the early 1800s. It is pure conjecture, but could the building with a belfry also shown on the 1650 map be the successor of the moated rectory, occupied by the Fakenham rector after the medieval rectory was abandoned and before the substantial Georgian building facing Oak Street was constructed?

The findings of this dig were not as informative as one would have wished and have not greatly increased our knowledge of the early history of Fakenham. A lack of artefacts and other dateable materials limited what could be deduced about the old rectory and its site. The location of the excavations on the site is shown on figure 6.12.

Two buildings were found on the 'island' enclosed by the moat. The first, adjacent to the southern part of the moat was timber-

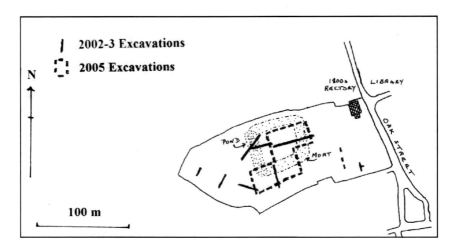

Fig. 6.12 Location of the excavations on the site of the old rectory
(from Wessex Archaeology 2006)

framed and supported by short flint, cobble and mortar walls. The floor was raised because of the wet ground upon which it was built. The construction was 'L-shaped' 30m long, 5m wide with a wing of 5m. Joist sockets were discovered in the walls and evidence of a garderobe (toilet) was found (Fig 6.13). The second building was constructed on the northern part of the 'island' and was slightly larger than the first. Like the first building, its base was made of flint and mortar with a timber superstructure; it may have been an extension, a partial replacement of the house, or possibly a barn. From the evidence revealed on site, the use of this building is uncertain.

An inspection trench was excavated across the moat on its north-eastern side and the cross-section is shown in figure 6.14. This indicates that the moat was dug down through the peat to the underlying solid rock, the chalk. What happened to the material dug out of the moat is unknown. The extension of the peat eventually covered a ditch of Roman age; a sample from the lowest layer of peat above the ditch gave a carbon date of 550 to 650 AD. It is thought an adjacent mass of stones may have been the foundation of a second bridge over the moat.

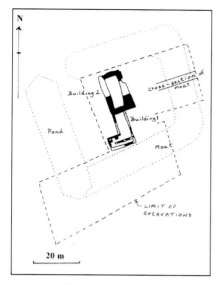

Fig. 6.13 Plan of the two buildings on the medieval rectory site (from Wessex Archaeology 2006)

In the succeeding years sedimentation in the moat took place, and the lowest layer of sediment (1) has preserved tree pollen from oak, hazel and alder with few grasses and weeds. In an upper layer (2), there is a sharp increase in pollen of grasses and weeds as well as cereals, specifically rye, and a decrease in tree pollen. This sequence suggests woodland clearance and development of agricultural activity in the surrounding countryside. Also found was the pollen of a cannabis species of plant, but it could be either hemp or hops as the pollen is very similar.

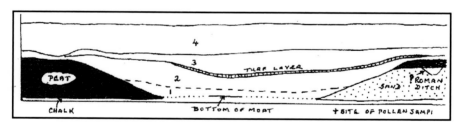

Fig. 6.14. Simplified cross-section of the moat.

Most of the moat had become completely filled with sediment by the 17th century and a buried turf line can be observed which was probably from a landscaped garden. Further flooding brought more identifiable layers of sediment (3) before modern layers of hardcore (4) for the garage premises which were previous occupants of the site.

References

Cornford, B. and Reid, A. 2005. 'The Uprising of 1381'. In: Ashwin, T. and Davison, A. 2005. An Historic Atlas of Norfolk. 3rd Edition. Phillimore.

Blomefield, F. 1805-10. The County of Norfolk. William Miller, London.

Brown, P. 1984. Domesday Book, Norfolk. Chichester

Cushion, B., Davison, A., Fenner, G., Goldsmith, R., Knight, J., Virgoe, N.,Wade, K., & Wade-Martins, P., 1982. 'Some deserted village sites in Norfolk' East Anglian Archaeology 14:40-101.

Darby, H.C. 1951. An Historical Geography of England Before AD 1800, C.U.P.

Dymond, D. 2005. 'Medieval and Later Markets'. In: Ashwin, T. and Davison, A. 2005. An Historic Atlas of Norfolk. 3rd Edition. Phillimore

Evans, N. 2005 'Worsted and Linen Weavers'. In: Ashwin, T. and Davison, A. 2005. An Historic Atlas of Norfolk. 3rd Edition. Phillimore.

Fitzjohn, P. 1956. The Story of Hempton. Wyman, Fakenham

Hoskins, W.G. 1958. 'History of Common land and Common Rights'. In: Royal Commission on Common Land, 1955-58, 149-166. Cmd.462. HMSO.

Nicholson, N.N. 1977. Hamatuna - Hempton.

Rutledge, E, 2005. 'Kett's rebellion, 1549'. In: Ashwin, T. and Davison, A. 2005. An Historic Atlas of Norfolk. 3rd Edition, Phillimore.

Wade-Martins, S. 1984. 'A History of Norfolk'. Phillimore, Chichester.

Wessex Archaeology, 2003. Oak Street Fakenham Norfolk: Archaeological Evaluation Report. Unpublished Report 53479.02

Wessex Archaeology, 2006. Moated Rectory at Oak Street Fakenham Norfolk: Report on the 2005 Excavation. Unpublished Report 591105

Yaxley, S., 'Men of Fakenham v. Big H 1520' in East Anglian Studies ed. A. Longcroft and R. Joby, Norwich 1995, Marwood

Chapter 7. The Changing Agricultural Scene

The manorial system, with its arable strips, commons and waste had given structure to rural life from Saxon times and throughout the medieval period. One disadvantage of the feudal system was that no benefit accrued to the individual for improving his land, consequently its fertility gradually deteriorated. Landowners began to realise that sole ownership of land could bring considerable benefits. From the early 17th century, some landowners began experimenting with new crops which had been tried on the continent; these required an enclosed space in which to grow and precluded the grazing of the common fields. Then there was a shortage of labour as villagers began the migration to the towns in search of higher wages. The commons themselves were subject to encroachments many of which were condoned, and the government of the time eventually saw fit to pass a General Enclosure Act in 1801. Wade-Martins (1984) quotes Kent (1796) that in 1796 two-thirds of Norfolk was in arable cultivation of which three-quarters was enclosed, and by 1830 most of the strips in the open fields had gone. However, for legal reasons, some fields remained in multiple ownership until the 1900s, the field to the north of the former Fakenham Grammar School being a case in point.

Enclosures were not without their social upheavals. The guide to Fakenham Parish Church mentions riots in Fakenham during the 16th century, and throughout the 17th and 18th century people throughout Britain were objecting to enclosures of common lands. In the final stages of enclosure, riots again took place in Fakenham in 1870 and the town pump was burnt when The Heath was finally enclosed.

The 17th and 18th centuries were unfortunate times for Fakenham as the town suffered from fire on three occasions. In 1660, following a fire in the town an appeal was read by royal command in churches all over England to repair their great loss by fire. Fires also occurred in 1718 and 1738. The report of the 1738 fire stated that 26 houses were destroyed but 'only the houses of the poor were affected and this was of no consequence'. This is certainly one reason why Fakenham does not have a core of medieval buildings such as can be seen in Walsingham. Additionally, the wealth which was accruing meant the buildings of the town centre were eventually replaced by more substantial brick and tile structures. In some cases a new façade was built on the front of an existing building, as may be seen in a building in Old Post Office Street.

In the countryside around Fakenham the enclosure of the open fields was accompanied by a wider movement of agricultural reform, rather than an 'agricultural revolution' as it has been described previously. Economically, the price of grain had increased during the Napoleonic wars and landowners and larger farmers were prospering. New approaches to farming were coming in and this was indicated by the formation of agricultural societies, cattle shows, sheep fairs, new implements, improvements to buildings and new crops. The leaders in this 'agricultural revolution' were people like Jethro Tull who invented the seed drill which sowed seed in rows and so made weeding easier; Bakewell of Dishley in Leicestershire who improved the quality of livestock, and locally Lord Townshend at Raynham became famous for promoting the growth of turnips in the Norfolk four-course rotation. Thomas Coke of Holkham, like Townshend, banished the fallow and brought the sandy lands into cultivation where formerly 'two rabbits fought over a blade of grass'. The activities of these local landowners were publicised by the like of Nathaniel Kent (1796) and Arthur Young (1804) who each published a General View of the Agriculture of the County of Norfolk for the Board of Agriculture.

The Great Estates

Historically, the upper echelons of society from the monarch downwards delighted in field sports and large areas of land were set aside for the purpose. In the 18th and 19th centuries the owners of large houses sought to aggrandise their estates by parkland, but they also bought significant areas to be farmed by tenant farmers. Faden's map of 1797 provides a partial picture of some of the estates at that time. The 19th century saw the consolidation of these estates in the Fakenham district under the great houses of Holkham, Houghton and Raynham. Wade Martins (2005) states that by the 1880s over half of Norfolk was in the hands of landowners with estates of over 1000 acres. These belonged to members of the aristocracy, members of the political elite of the time as well as gentlemen farmers at the less esteemed end of the social spectrum. The Holkham estate with 43,000 acres was the largest, followed by Raynham with 18,000 acres and Houghton with 15,000 acres. In addition there were eight estates of over 10,000 acres located mainly in north-west Norfolk.

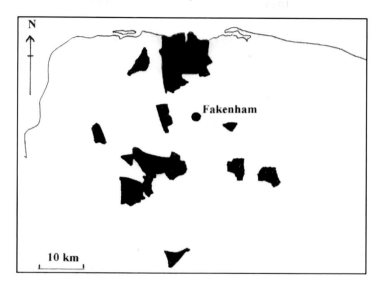

Fig.7.1 Extent of the Holkham Estate

The Coke family had purchased Holkham in 1659, moving from the (later deserted) village of Godwick. Subsequently, Thomas William Coke who became the first Earl of Leicester, was a member of Parliament for Norfolk from 1776 to 1806 and again from 1807 to 1832. He greatly extended the farming activities of his estate and became famous for the improvements he made to his lands, his crops and livestock. The change from open heath to the landscape we see today was accomplished by a number of different means.

The manorial system had been under pressure from environmental and social reasons which resulted in the gradual enclosure of the common fields, eliminating multiple ownership. Once enclosed, improvement could take place and the main process was that of 'marling'. In Chapter 1, it was pointed out that beneath the sandy topsoil of north Norfolk was a chalky clay left by one of the glacial episodes. Spreading this calcareous clay on the surface checked the acidity and added moisture-holding clay to the soil. Thus almost every field in the Fakenham district has a marl pit, although many have been infilled with farm waste in recent times.

A second major component in the reclamation from heath was the livestock. The extensive fold course system of sheep pasturage with hardy, black-faced Norfolk Horn sheep was replaced by faster maturing Leicester and Southdown breeds which were folded onto the enclosed lands so their droppings fertilized the land and added organic matter to the sandy soils. In the late 18th century stockyards were built in which the cattle were over-wintered on turnips and bedded on straw, providing copious quantities of manure for the fields. These improvements, combined with the Norfolk four-course rotation, including turnips and clovers (which added nitrogen to the soil), enabled greatly increased crop yields to be obtained before the days of artificial fertilisers. The standard of cattle and sheep breeds were also improved as stock did not have to be slaughtered in the autumn. These techniques were spread amongst the farming community by Coke at his 'Sheep Shearings', held at Holkham between the 1770s and 1821.

Charles, the Second Viscount Townshend of Raynham, was born in 1674 and died in 1738. After a successful career including being a Privy Councillor, Ambassador to the States of Holland, Secretary of State and Lord President of the Council, he retired from politics in 1730. According to Wade Martins (1990), he was regarded politically as a safe pair of hands during the change-over in 1714 from the Stuarts to the Hanoverians. Retiring to Norfolk, he concentrated on improving the estate which he inherited in 1687. In the time of his father, Horatio, most of the lands on the estate were still farmed in medieval strips but the movement for enclosure had begun and with longer leases to tenants the communal lands gradually were enclosed.

Charles Townshend extended the work his father had begun and by the use of marling, hedging, ditching and where necessary under drainage brought unprofitable land into profitable farms. The longer leases he granted increasingly stipulated the use of turnips instead of the traditional fallow in the 'Norfolk' four-course rotation of crops. He therefore became known as 'Turnip' Townshend.

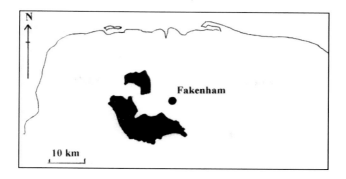

Fig. 7.2 Extent of the Raynham Estate

Sheep were also an important part of the Raynham farming enterprise, especially on the lighter lands of Coxford, Creake, Stiffkey and Rudham but around the turn of the century (1700) increasingly the fold-courses were sub-let and enclosed. (Wade Martins, 1990). Falling prices for wool probably helped to re-enforce the changes.

At Houghton, Townshend's contemporary, Walpole, who had become George I's chief Minister, was occupied in a similar manner improving his estate. Formerly, the country from Holkham to Houghton had been described as 'a wild sheep walk before the spirit of improvement seized the inhabitants'. The countryside was now dominated by 'enclosures cultivated in a most husband-like manner, richly manured, well peopled and yielding 100 times the produce that it did in the former state'.

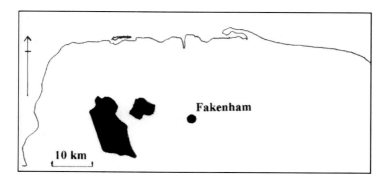

Fig.7.3 Extent of the Houghton Estate

These changes in the agriculture and landscape of our region did not take place overnight. Conservative attitudes resisted innovations, as happened with the seed drill, even when it was well-publicised by Jethro Tull in his book Horse-hoeing Husbandry. A surplus of labour allowed some Norfolk farmers to continue sowing broadcast up to the 1750s and hand-dibbling until the 1840s (Wade Martins, 2002).

In the years before these changes took place, Norfolk was not renowned as an agricultural county, as large areas remained unproductive. A last glimpse of this former landscape is given by Faden (1797) on his map of Norfolk where in north-west Norfolk many roads are shown passing over unfenced heathland. Some of the roads or tracks shown by Faden were subsequently down-graded or abandoned when the enclosure acts were passed and rectangular fields became the norm.

The coastal ports of Lynn, Wells, Cley and Blakeney all benefited from this improved agriculture as surpluses of grain were produced and exported. Inland, Fakenham was developing as the focal point for the surrounding region. After becoming part of the Duchy of Lancaster in 1377, the Manor of Fakenham belonged successively to the Cokes, the Calthorpes, the L'Estranges, and Lee Warners and finally to the Jones family which has held the title of Lord of the Manor ever since. The Gwynn family, which came to Fakenham in 1613, became a large landowner in Fakenham based upon Baron's Hall which they had bought in 1593. Only the barn of this farm remains today as a new Baron's Hall, constructed in 1804, which survives to the present day. The Gwynn family remained owners of Baron's Hall until shortly after the First World War.

In concluding this section on agricultural change, an important role was played by Sir George Edwards. He was born in 1850 and rose from being a farm boy to become a Member of Parliament. He is remembered for his work in founding and running a union for agricultural workers. Knighted by King George V, he lived in Hempton, and latterly in Fakenham. He died in 1933, is buried in Queen's Road cemetery and commemorated on the town sign.

In the late 18th and 19th centuries, the road pattern in Fakenham gradually changed. The Gwynns blocked the former road to Norwich, now known as Old Lane, forcing people to use the road further north now known as Norwich Road. A western approach to the town along Hall Staithe became less important and following the construction of the bridge in 1833, Bridge Street became the preferred southern entry to the town rather than the narrow Mill Lane and Tunn Street. With the Market place as a focus, the two inns became stopping points for coaches to London and Norwich.

Toll roads

During the Medieval period, it was often the monastic institutions which assumed responsibility for maintenance of the roads. A local illustration of this was the little priory of Hempton having responsibility for the causeway between Hempton and Fakenham. As we have seen, that caused friction between the citizens of Fakenham and the Prior. After the Dissolution of the Monasteries, parishes were made responsible by a statute of 1555. This was not particularly successful and the results amateurish, even after it became possible to levy rates for the purpose in 1691. In the 17th century Turnpike Acts were introduced by the government, which

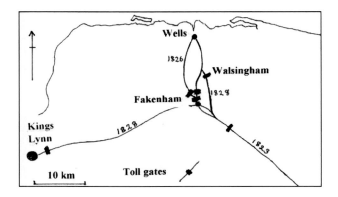

Fig. 7.4 Toll roads in the Fakenham district

appointed trustees who were empowered to erect toll gates, collect tolls and maintain the highway. The invention in 1816 by John McAdam of a new surface for roads, made with granite chippings bound with tar, came a little too late for the turnpikes as within a few years, the railway had superseded the roads for fast movement of people and goods.

65

Fakenham had to wait until the beginning of the 19th century before any roads were turnpiked (Davison and Joby, 2005, Robinson and Rose, 2008). The Fakenham to Norwich road was turnpiked in 1823, followed by the 'dry' road to Wells in 1826. Before demolition, the toll bar cottages used to stand at the crossroads where Sandy Lane met Wells Road, and a toll cottage east of Walsingham still stands in the woods just before the road forks to either Thursford or Little Snoring.. The King's Lynn road joined the system in 1828 as did the road to Walsingham from Langor Bridge. As has been found at the present time, improved roads result in more traffic and maintenance problems increased accordingly. It is almost certain that the first coal supplied for Fakenham's new gasworks came by the turnpike from the harbour at Wells, having completed a sea journey from the Northumberland coalfield.

The most significant factor in the development of Fakenham was the market which brought people in from the surrounding villages every week on Thursday. The commercial skills of families such as the Peckovers enabled Fakenham to become a centre for banking and merchandising, the first bank being opened in 1782. As will be seen in the next chapter, the town became the focus for many other trades which supported the surrounding agricultural area. The money brought into the town enabled the reconstruction of many houses in the Georgian style. From medieval times Fakenham had a Market Cross, a raised rectangular building which was found to be unsafe in 1800 and pulled down. The Market Cross was replaced by a sundial and prison cage. These were sited where the cinema now stands, a building built as a Corn Hall in 1855.

Across the river from Fakenham, Hempton took on the form it retains to the present day with the buildings fronting Dereham road, The Green and Back street. A second focal point was the cross roads on the western side of the Green. A farm close to the site of the old priory, called Abbey farm, was situated on the eastern side of Dereham road as was a building known as the Bridewell, both now demolished. Misdemeanours in the past were dealt with harshly, especially when they affected the upper levels of the social hierarchy. Such a 'house of correction' was built in Hempton of which nothing remains. Called the 'Bridewell', it took its name from a house of correction in London situated by a well adjacent to the church of St

Bride. Prisons were dreadful places before the prison reform movement of John Howard (1726-1790) but through his efforts some humanity was introduced into the system. A glimpse into the life of such an institution may be obtained by a visit to the Walsingham Bridewell which is included on historical walks around the village.

References

Davison, A. and Joby, R. 2005. 'Early Roads and Turnpiles'. In: Ashwin T.and Davison, A. 2005. An Historic Atlas of Norfolk. 3rd Edition. Phillimore.

Faden, W. 1797 . A Topographical Map of the County of Norfolk. Reprint, Larks Press.

Kent, N. 1796. General View of the Agriculture of Norfolk.

Robinson, B. and Rose, E.J. 2008. Norfolk Origins 2 Roads and Tracks. Poppyland Publishing. Cromer.

Wade Martins, S. 1990. Turnip Townshend: Statesman and Farmer. Poppyland Publishing.

Wade Martins, S. 1984. A History of Norfolk. Phillimore, Chichester.

Wade Martins, S. 2002. Changing Agriculture in Georgian and Victorian Norfolk. Norfolk Origins 6, Poppyland Publishing, Cromer.

Wade Martins, S. 2005. Great Estates in the 19th Century. In: Ashwin, T. and Davison, A. 2005. An Historic Atlas of Norfolk. 3rd Edition. Phillimore.

Young, A. 1804. A General View of the Agriculture of Norfolk. Board of Agriculture, London.

Chapter 8. Industrial development

While all the great agricultural improvements were taking place in the countryside around Fakenham, the town was steadily consolidating itself as the central market for the whole surrounding area. Inevitably, this meant provision of services to the villages and agriculture. In addition to a range of shops, providing food and other necessities for the whole population, the town became a centre of industry based on metals and milling. The blacksmith was a vital member of the community from the Bronze Age onwards, and the practice of milling took place from early times. Later, other industries, such as printing, came in to diversify the town's activities.

Milling

Three mills were recorded in Fakenham by the Domesday survey. By the 16th century there were only two mills and when the mill southeast of the town on Maltmoor, ceased to operate there was only one remaining. The Maltmoor mill was almost certainly sited where the track from Testerton crossed the river, a place now dominated by the three brick arches of the former LNER railway. (A water mill must be situated on a river, and for corn to be brought to it for milling, a road is required).

At Fakenham mill, the river was diverted to the northern side of the flood plain to provide a drop of about a metre to power a water wheel. The diversionary dam also enabled the miller to store water upstream of the mill; it also provided a dry passage across the swampy valley floor. This dam may still be seen alongside the road from Fakenham to Hempton. The river here was previously almost double its present width, but when the mill changed to steam power, it was neglected and became filled with sediment. Eventually, the river bed was partly infilled and the area planted with trees and grass. The present Fakenham Mill was constructed around 1720 probably on the site of a former mill as the diversion is shown on the 1650 map. It was enlarged in 1863 and steam power introduced in 1885 and conversion to electric power took place in the early 20th century. The mill ceased to grind corn in 1980, and was converted into attractive flats in 1982 (Fig. 8.1).

Fig. 8.1 Fakenham Mill (Photo E.M.Bridges)

Hempton's watermill, known as Goggs' Mill, was built in the early 18th century and the earliest reference to it was in 1721. The mill was later owned by Thomas Goggs (1827-1913) who lived in the large house called The Grove in Fakenham. The son of the vicar of South Creake, he was clearly quite well-off and left money 'to the poor widows and aged persons of Fakenham and Hempton to be expended in the purchase of coals for the benefit of such persons'. Details of the mill's history have been lost as there were no deeds available when the Water Board acquired the mill in 1951. A picture taken in the 1890s shows the mill in good condition (Fig. 8.2), but by the beginning of the First World War it had ceased operation; by the 1940s the mill and the cottage attached to it were ruinous. It was finally demolished in 1954. Proposals for a tea room and swimming pool in the inter-war years came to nought, but the mill pond was used by children as a swimming pool during the war years (as the author remembers).

In 1781, the owner of Fakenham Mill, William Green, was granted permission to build a windmill on The Heath, at a place called Windmill Hill, implying that it had previously been the site

Fig.8.2. Goggs (Hempton) Mill
(Photo Fakenham Local History Society)

of a windmill. Another windmill was built at White Post, near the junction of Holt and Greenway roads. This was indicated on a one-inch to one mile map, published by Faden in 1797, which preceded the first of the Ordnance Survey maps. Nothing exists of these windmills at the present day. The stump of a windmill may be seen off Holt Road, near to the entrance of the former Junior School. This was built as a smock mill in 1836 and converted into a tower mill in 1849. Fifteen years later its top was blown off in a gale, since when it has been used as a house. Bryant's map (1824-6) shows windmills both on the western side of Hempton Green on a site now built over, and on the eastern side at the site of the former Abbey farm. In the 20th century, Hempton's windmill is also worth a comment as it was a landmark until the Second World War when it was demolished because it was thought to be a marker for the Luftwaffe, directing their planes to Raynham airfield! First documented in 1827, the mill was probably built around 1820 and at that time belonged to a John Jarrett of Abbey Farm; after he died the mill was owned by his wife as is recorded in White's Directory of 1836. Like Fakenham's windmill, it suffered damage in a gale, with part of the sails carried by the wind as far as The Bell public house (Fig. 8.3).

Fig. 8.3 Hempton windmill
(Photo Fakenham Local History Society)

Iron working

The history of iron working goes back to Iron Age times, but as far as Fakenham is concerned, no evidence exists of medieval or earlier iron working. Evidence of metal-working of the middle Saxon period exists in the surrounding area, particularly near Rudham, Hindringham and to the south of the town. Horses would have required shoes and so the blacksmith must have played his part in the unrecorded life of Fakenham throughout the ages. In the 19th and early 20th century, there were three blacksmiths in Fakenham and one in Hempton. The Fakenham blacksmiths' premises were located in Nelson Road (H.H.Piercy), a yard off Oak Street (George and Balls) and in Quaker Lane (James Wakefield). The Hempton blacksmith (E.J. Huggins) was in the building adjacent to the offices of Fishers the builders.

A small foundry, owned by Mr Clare Bowles was situated in a yard on the east side of Bridge Street; the observant will notice that some drain gratings in the town have the name C. Bowles inscribed upon them; he also made the iron pens for the cattle market, some of which remain in the car park adjacent to Miller's walk (Fig. 8.4).

Bowles was also a brass and tin plate worker, bell hanger, gas fitter and coppersmith according to an advertisement in an almanac for 1888.

Fig.8.4. Ironwork by Clare Bowles of Fakenham
(Left) Wrought ironwork of pens at the cattle market
(Below) Drain grating from Mill Lane

(Photos E.M.Bridges)

A much larger ironworks, known as the Farmers Foundry grew up at Great Ryburgh on the other side of the railway from the Maltings. The railway brought in coal and pig iron but there was no specific siding for the foundry. The foundry was started by a group of local farmers under the name of St Andrew's Works and in 1890 it became the Farmers Foundry. It is graphically described by Dick Joice (1991) in his book Full Circle where he describes the moulders carefully making the sand moulds, the crucible in which the iron was made and the tapping of the crucible which sent a river of molten iron into the prepared sand moulds. Everything was done by hand, loading the layers of scrap, pig iron, coke and chalk into the crucible. Ploughs, rollers, cultivators, water carts, elevators and iron-wheeled hurdles for penning sheep were made. In the machine shop more precise engineering took place with the construction of mobile engines, suitable for driving threshing tackle, an example of which is in the Bygones Collection at Holkham.

Other foundries in the Fakenham district included those at Great Walsingham, Sculthorpe, Burnham, Binham and Wells. As a footnote to the working of metals in the Fakenham area, mention must be made of the South Creake Razor Blade factory (Durst, 2005). This works was in a former brewery that was in operation until 1925. The buildings were bought in that year by Mr George Money who set about making razor blades. The Ace Razor Blade Company made blades from a continuous strip of metal from which the blades were punched, hardened, and sharpened using machinery designed and made by Money himself. The works was sold in 1972. It is interesting to note that Money also patented a process for making cornflakes marketed as 'Myflakes'. Surprisingly, another brand of cornflakes was patented by a Mr Alley, also of South Creake, as 'Farmers Glory' which was successful until forced off the market by larger businesses.

Brickyards, sand and gravel pits, quarries
Nineteenth century maps indicate that there were four brickyards in the immediate vicinity of Fakenham. At Claypit Lane, the flooded clay pit remained until after the second world war, but subsequently it has been filled in and is now a bus depot. Other brickyards are shown on the 1885 1:10560 scale Ordnance Survey Map. On Greenway Lane, fronted by Greenway Terrace was a brickworks with several buildings, but the map does not specifically indicate where a kiln was situated. Immediately to the north, on Grove Lane, a smaller brickworks with kiln is indicated. By 1906 neither of these works is shown to be operational.

A sandpit was opened on the east side of Sandy Lane, but ceased to produce sand before the Second World War. It is now Olivia Close. Several gravel pits were opened to the south of Hempton Green and across the Dereham Road at a site called Flagmoor. Also in Hempton a brickyard was situated on Shereford Road on a site now occupied by Batterby Close. A substantial brickyard was situated north-east of the village of Barney which supplied bricks for the construction of the Fakenham printing works.

The underlying chalk rock was mined in quarries at Cley,

Walsingham and also east of Wells where it was used for agricultural lime. Chalk was obtained from Broomsthorpe for foundation material for the runways at RAF Scunthorpe (Baldwin, 1999). The brickworks which provided all the bricks for the wall around the Holkham estate was situated at Peterstone. Many aggregate quarries were opened during the second world war to provide gravel for making concrete runways for the several RAF stations in the area.

Coming of the Railways

In the 19th century, the whole country was opened up by the spread of the railway network. Norfolk lagged behind in the process, only beginning in 1844 with the Yarmouth to Norwich railway. Other lines built by local companies followed, and were swallowed up by the Eastern Counties Railway in 1854, which in turn became the Great Eastern Railway in 1864. The first railway to serve Fakenham came from Norwich via Wymondham and Dereham and opened on 20th March, 1849. A 'temporary' terminus was constructed which served as the station throughout the life of this railway (Fig. 8.5).

Fig.8.5 Fakenham East Station (LNER)
(Photo E.M.Bridges)

This was situated where Fayre Green is today. Two problems were encountered in the immediate Fakenham area which delayed progress of the line onwards to Wells, these were the crossing of the river

Wensum valley and immediately to the north of the town a long deep cutting was required. Spoil from the cutting provided material to build an embankment from the Ryburgh area and a bridge with three brick arches was required to span the river itself.

Further problems were experienced near East Barsham where the line crosses the River Stiffkey. A tunnel was dug to take the railway through the hills north of the river, but because of the unconsolidated nature of the ground a collapse took place and a deep cutting had to be used instead. Eventually, the line reached Wells in 1857 where a more respectable terminus was constructed, although somewhat short of the original proposals, which led to the former Railway Hotel being some distance from the railway itself.

The crossing of the river Stiffkey near East Barsham was the site of an incident when flooding, on 26th August, 1912, undermined the bridge and a derailment occurred. Another accident occurred at 9.37 a.m. in Fakenham Station on 27th May, 1931 when a train from

Fig.8.6. Rail crash at Fakenham, 1831
(Photo Fakenham Local History Society)

Norwich to Wells ran into a train heading in the opposite direction standing in the station. One person was killed and twelve injured. Both engines were derailed and the wooden coaches were telescoped into each other (Fig. 8.6).

A second line came to Fakenham from King's Lynn in 1880, and was extended to Melton Constable where it linked with routes to Norwich, Cromer and North Walsham. It began life as the Lynn and

Fakenham Railway but eventually became the Midland and Great Northern Railway. Compared with the single track line from Norwich to Wells, this was a grander affair with double tracks and a well appointed station, situated not in Fakenham but in Hempton. This line provided connections to the Midlands and the north of England. There was no connection between the two Fakenham lines, which crossed at different levels south-east of the town and the two stations lying over a mile apart.

The railways played an important role during the Second World War when they provided transport for heavy goods unsuited to the narrow country roads of the time. They also carried the military personnel who staffed the many airfields and coastal defences. They were responsible for carrying fuel; both stations had a depot for coal and the eastern station had a Shell oil depot as well. Cattle, sheep and farm produce were also carried; both stations had cattle pens. The LNER line in particular, provided a link for the maltings at Ryburgh and Fakenham to the port facilities at Wells.

After the war ended, the railways continued for a while, but their service was no contest for local buses and the increasing car ownership which allowed people to travel when and where they wanted rather than where the trains took them. Inevitably the parlous state of the railway's finances and the review of services carried out by Dr Beeching in 1964-8 resulted in cuts. The link between Fakenham and Lynn had already been lost in 1959 and passenger services were withdrawn from the LNER line from May 10th, 1964 and the line finally closed to all traffic in 1979. The station was demolished in September, 1984.

Nothing remains of the Fakenham East station buildings, but to the north of Norwich Road, extending as far as Greenway Lane the former deep cutting has been made into a footpath. Part of the Fakenham Town station platform has been preserved on the forecourt of the Jewson building supplies depot. A massive concrete buffer remains at the corner of Goggs Mill Road and Back Street adjacent to the Garden Centre. Eastwards, the path of the former railway has been utilised as the access road to the Sports Centre and Racecourse and westward as far as Shereford, the former track of the railway has been made into a footpath.

Wood Working

Until shortly after the Second World War, Fakenham had two wood yards, one on Summerhill (Clarke) and the other on Holt Road. (Smith). Both supplied sawn timber for a wide range of uses and the Summerhill yard retained facilities for the construction of farm vehicles, although infrequently used, until the 1950s.

Malting and brewing

Conversion of barley into malt for the brewing industry has been part of rural industry for many centuries and formerly most East Anglian towns would have had a maltings; in this respect Fakenham was no exception. An old malthouse was situated in the angle between the Church Lanes and Highfield road. Now part of Candler's Funeral Parlour premises, only some of the outer walls remain. The same buildings were also used as a tannery.

The largest of Fakenham's maltings, run by the Dewing family, was situated alongside the Eastern Railway Station on the site now occupied by the Maltings Care Home (Fig. 8.7). Some half dozen men were employed in the malting process. Barley grains are first

Fig. 8.7 Fakenham Maltings
(Photo Fakenham Local History Society)

steeped in water for 2 to 3 days to obtain sufficient moisture for germination to commence. Next the moistened barley is placed on the malting floor and warmed to between 55 and 62°F. To ensure an

77

even heating the grain had to be turned regularly by large-bladed malt shovels. Maltings had thick walls and small windows to enable the conditions in which the malt was made to be uniform. Finally, the temperature was raised in a drying kiln to stop further germination and to drive off any excess moisture. By this process, the starch in the grain is converted by an enzyme diastase into maltose and dextrin. The dried malt is crushed between steel rollers and is then known as 'grist' which is supplied to the brewer to make beer.

A brewery was located in Hall Staithe under the name of Charlton's; their malt house remains, and an example of one of their beer bottles is in Fakenham Museum. This brewery ceased production and was partly demolished in 1912. An earlier brewery was located on Hayes lane, formerly known as Brewery Lane.

It is necessary to return to Great Ryburgh for the only remaining maltings in the Fakenham area. The key to the successful location of this works was the railway, which, when completed to Wells, enabled grain and malt to be carried easily to the port facilities on Wells quay. It also enabled coal to be brought from the coalfields to fire the furnaces which heated the floors of the malt house. The process completed, the malt was sent off to be made into beer, or if of very best quality, into whisky.

In addition to the former coaching inns, Fakenham was well provided with pubs, reflecting its significance as a market town (Baldwin, 1982). The oldest of these was the Royal Oak in Oak Street, which with the Star and the Sun (formerly in Norwich Street) were owned by Charlton who ran the brewery in Hall Staithe. More than a dozen other pubs were open during the 19th and 20th centuries. The Cattle Market Tavern on Wells Road was so named because of the adjacent pig market which closed in 1882; it was amalgamated with the new cattle market opened in 1857 in Chapel Street, now called Cattle Market Street. The Victoria on Victoria Lane was opened in the 1880s to cater for the navvies building the railway line to Melton Constable; it closed in 1914. The Railway Tavern and the Great Eastern were situated on Norwich Road en route to the station. Lord Nelson was commemorated by the Nelson in Nelson Road and the Anchor in Holt Road possibly is associated with the name of Seppings, who figures on the town sign.

There were three pubs in Hempton but only The Bell survives.

Records of the Buck Inn, formerly at the western end of Horns Row show it had facilities for brewing, and it is almost certain that the King's Head did as well. These pubs have a long history, dating back to the 1600s. Interestingly, an 18th century owner of the Bell was stated to be a weaver, although the immediate Fakenham area was not much involved in the medieval weaving trade.

Printing

Fakenham was unusual in that it developed an industry which was not related to agriculture, this was printing (Baldwin & Baldwin, 2002). It arose from the activities of a few individuals at the beginning of the 19th century. The first of these was Chadley Stewardson who moved from Norwich in 1803, where he was a Freeman. The earliest piece of his work which has survived is from 1819, but he was known to be producing stage-coach posters at an earlier date. The business was taken over by his son George in 1851 who also developed a stationery shop. George Stewardson was responsible for building over the passage from the upper market to the Church in 1860 (Fig.8.8). He died in 1886 and the business passed to his son who died in 1897, leaving the business to his two sisters. In 1903, H.F. Andrews left Miller, Son & Co to work as the printer at Stewardsons, he continued as a jobbing printer until after the Second World War, producing business cards, wedding, baptism and funeral cards, posters, slate club cards, bill heads for businesses in the town and the locally-produced part of the parish magazine. Printing ceased on the site after H.F. Andrews bought The Lancaster Press in 1948 when his son returned from war service. Stewardson's book and stationery shop continued until 2000 when it was merged into the Aldiss department store (Fig. 8.8).

Secondly, Sampson Pratt and his brother came from North Elmham in the late 1800s and, after working in the coach-building trade, decided to set up a seed merchant's business in the Upper Market. By 1900 they had moved their business to White Horse Street. It is thought they may have had a press to print seed packets.

Fig. 8.8 Stewardsons
the shop below the church tower
(Photo E.M.Bridges)

Thirdly, Thomas Miller was a printer and grocer in Wells before moving to Fakenham in 1845, where he set-up a business in the Lower Market. He published a newspaper called The Fakenham Advertiser and then in 1858 purchased a property on the north side of Norwich Street. In 1869, he expanded into the property next door and dealt in earthenware goods before trans-forming his enterprise into Miller's Royal Bazaar. In this shop bedsteads, mattresses, fenders and fire irons, knives and forks, clocks and watches were advertised in 1888. His son took over his father's printing interests and moved into a building built by his father on the south side of Norwich Street. Thomas junior at first rented the building, but by the 1880s had extended the building across the rear access lane and installed several Wharfedale printing presses, calling his enterprise The Wharfedale Works. By the turn of the century there were some 200 employees working for Miller. However, by 1908 the business was in financial trouble and was taken over by Wyman & Sons, but it continued under the Miller name. The printing works offices fronted on to Norwich Street (Fig. 8.9).

Wymans continued the expansion of the printing works until it occupied most of the west side of White Horse Street. During a fire in 1914, an overhead walkway had to be demolished to stop the fire spreading from the Wharfedale Works to the Norwich Street premises. Molten lead was said to be flowing down the street at the height of the fire. In 1929, Miller, Son & Co. were wound up and completely absorbed into Wymans. The eastern side of Whitehorse

Fig.8.9 Printing Works Offices before demolition.
(Photo Fakenham Local History Society)

Street was occupied by small cottages until after the Second World War, but progressively these were demolished for printing works extensions. In the 1950s, Wymans' directors purchased all the companies interests and set up Cox and Wyman Ltd. with the Eagle Star Insurance Company as backers. Expansion of the works took place with the two-storey Eagle Star building on the east side of Whitehorse Street being constructed to house a compositing room, but it actually became a bindery.

At this stage there was no further room to expand on the site and in the 1960s Cox and Wyman Ltd. were taken over by Thomas Tilling. A Crawley-based litho printers, Bookprint, was moved lock, stock and barrel to Fakenham to occupy a new building on Old Lane (now the Aldiss superstore). Opened in 1970, this building enabled the staff to be increased to around 600 people. With the changing techniques of printing, the old letterpress printing machines were superseded and the old Wharfedale Works emptied. Competition from overseas and little support from government at home, made the works unprofitable and after being bought by Richard Clay of Bungay and re-named The Fakenham Press, Fakenham's major industry was closed in 1982. A commemorative plaque may be seen on the wall of the Argos store.

Closure of the Fakenham Press was a body-blow to the town, but many of the former Press staff met the challenge and set-up small businesses of their own. These include Fakenham Photosetting, Dickens Print Trade Finishers, The Kayleigh Press, Norton and Moyes, Norwood Printing and the Iceni Press. The Iceni Press merged with the Lancaster Press in 1995 to form the Lanceni Press and in 2009 it became Newprint and Design.

Newspapers
Another feature of Fakenham's printing industry was the production of newspapers. The Norfolk Chronicle began life in Norwich in 1761 and after moving to Holt, was printed by Rounce and Wortley at North Walsham. As Baldwin & Baldwin (2002) describes, several editions were being printed, one of which was The Fakenham Post. This newspaper was bought by Thomas Cook of Sennowe Hall in 1936 and brought to Fakenham where it was printed in a wooden building, now demolished, on Chronicle Lane, off Norwich Road. The Norfolk Chronicle lasted until 1957 when it was absorbed into the Dereham and Fakenham Times.

In 1879, E.W. Southwood, a relation of the Miller family, began the production of The Fakenham and Dereham Times in 1879, and he is listed in a Directory of 1886 as being the publisher. This paper survived until 1957 when both it and the Norfolk Chronicle were bought by The Norfolk News Company and incorporated into their Dereham and Fakenham Times. A Fakenham and Wells edition of this paper is published but does not fully represent Fakenham as it is dominated by events in Dereham. In order to fill the gap a very successful venture, financed by advertising, has been the Fakenham Sun, edited by Barry Hawkes and printed by the Lanceni Press (now Newprint and Design). The parish magazine, The Beacon, formerly produced by H.F. Andrews at Stewardson's, and latterly by Lanceni Press, continues to serve the church members, but also the wider community.

Coach building and motor engineering

Earlier, it has been mentioned that the blacksmiths of the town provided a service for all metallic requirements and, with the wood yards, were largely responsible for the construction and maintenance of farm carts and machinery as well as other horse-drawn vehicles. Southgates, in Oak Street, was established in 1825 as a coach builder but gradually changed to motor vehicles in the early years of the 20th century to become main Ford agents by 1914. They continued their work with farm machinery and tractors and were eventually taken over by R.C. Edmondson. By the end of the 20th century, the site was derelict and is now the location of a Tesco supermarket.

The firm of Baxters were the first engineers dealing solely with motor cars in the town, opening in 1891 in premises on Holt Road. Others followed in the 1910s and 1920s. These included Blake and Howard on Wells Road, Massey and Bridges, and Carleys on Norwich Road. Blake continued until his death in 1979 but Howard moved to Quaker Lane and concentrated on motor cycles. Carleys also sold motorcycles, taking over from John White who had similar interests. Their Norwich Road site is now occupied by Howes.

Fig. 8.10 Massey and Bridges garage.
(Photo Fakenham Local History Society)

The garage occupied by Pom Blake formerly belonged to John Garrood whose inventions led to greatly improved cycles, using tubular metal forks for the wheels and more effective pedals. He also accepted a challenge to make an automatic paper-feeder for the Wharfedale printing presses of Thomas Miller. Garrood is represented on the town sign by a penny farthing cycle.

The firm of Massey and Bridges began life as a taxi firm with Blake and Howard, then moved to the Crown Inn's barn in Bridge Street and in the early 1920s built their own premises opposite Fakenham Mill (Fig. 8.10). The two partners had became friends in the trenches during the first world war and after demobilisation set up in business together (Bridges, 1998). After being agents for Renault for a few years, they eventually became main Austin agents for the Fakenham area. The firm continued until 1955 when it was sold by the partners to Mann Egerton of Norwich, under whose management it did not prosper. It passed from being a depot for fruit machines to a billiard hall and was eventually knocked down for housing. Massey Close and Bridges Walk recall the names of the two partners of this former Fakenham enterprise.

Gas production
At the end of the 18th century, William Murdoch invented the

Fig. 8.11. Fakenham Gas Works Museum
(Photo E.M.Bridges)

84

process for the manufacture of gas from coal which could be used to provide a much improved light compared with oil lamps and candles. The first gas works was built in London around 1810 and the benefits of street lighting rapidly spread across England. In Fakenham, a group of local business men floated a company in 1846 called The Fakenham Gas Company, in order to light the streets after dark. A site near Fakenham Mill was chosen and the first retorts installed (Bridges, 2009). This took place three years before the coming of the railway, so the coal required must have been brought overland from Wells by farm cart. The works was reconstructed in the late 1880s and again in 1910, the structure which remains to the present day. Gas production continued from 1846 until the works closed in 1965, after which the town was supplied from Norwich before conversion to natural gas in the 1970s. At its closure, the gasworks served over 500 homes, used three railway wagon loads of coal a week and employed between eight and twelve people. The redundant gas works was simply locked and left. Surprisingly it was not vandalised, nor was the equipment taken away for scrap and by the 1980s it was realised that Fakenham's gas works was the only complete works in England that had not been demolished. Consequently, at the behest of the Norfolk Industrial Archaeological Society, it was declared an ancient monument grade two, and in 1987 it became Fakenham Museum of Gas and Local History (Bridges, 2009). As a result, Fakenham has a unique piece of Britain's industrial history and an attraction which draws interested visitors from all over Britain and abroad (Fig. 8.11).

Seed merchants

As a rural market town, Fakenham and its weekly market served the surrounding local district for virtually all its needs. One of these was the provision of seeds for the many farms. The largest firm was Sheringham and Overman, whose offices were in the Square where Woolworth's now stands. This firm can be traced back to the Peckover family in 1657 and was the oldest business in town when it closed. By the 1950s, they had built much larger premises on Holt Road which subsequently became a Co-operative supermarket and now the site is occupied by Lidl. Other seed merchants in town in the 1930s included E. Burrage in Bridge Street, Cannel & Sons, also in

Bridge Street, R. Gray at the LNER Station, R.J. Seaman & Sons, also at the LNER station, Stark & Sons, Norwich Street and W. Wright & Son.

References

Anon 2005. The Railways of Norfolk. Norwich Evening News Publication.

Baldwin, J. 1982. Fakenham: Town on the Wensum. Poppyland Publishing, Cromer.

Baldwin, J. & Baldwin M. 2002.   A Good Impression: The story of printing in Fakenham. Baldwin, Fakenham.

Baldwin, J. (ed) 1999. RAF Sculthorpe: 50 years of watching and waiting. Baldwin, Fakenham

Bridges, E.M. 1998. Massey and Bridges: A Brief History of a Fakenham Firm. Fakenham Museum.

Bridges, E.M. 2009. History of Fakenham Museum of Gas and Local History. Fakenham Museum.

Durst, D. 2005. 'The South Creake Razor Blade Factory'. Journal of the Norfolk Industrial Archaeological Society 7; No 5 59-66

Joice, D. 1991. Full Circle. Boydell Press, Woodbridge.

Chapter 9. Growth of the town

In the earlier chapters of this book we have seen how from small beginnings in the Saxon times, Fakenham has grown to become a focal point in central North Norfolk. From an estimated population of between 100 and 150 at the time of the Domesday Survey, until the first accurate, detailed maps were compiled, the built-up area of the town scarcely extended beyond Oak Street and Norwich Street with a small cluster of buildings south of the market place in the centre.

In the census of 1801, the population of the town is given as 1,236 and fifty years later it had grown to almost double that figure (2,240). Growth continued up to 1911 when just over 3,000 inhabitants were counted, but in the following three decades it decreased to 2,843. No census was taken during the Second World War but in the five decades since 1951 the population has increased by around a thousand people per decade. At the millennium, Fakenham's population stood at about 8,000 (Fig.9.1). Published plans for the future identify the town as a focal point for further growth.

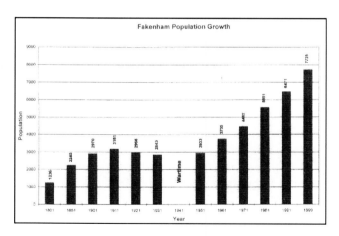

Fig. 9.1. Fakenham - growth of population 1801-2000

The early structure of the settlement of Fakenham was similar to what may still be seen in the ground plans of the abandoned villages such as Godwick or Pudding Norton. Each plot within the settlement had sufficient land around it to form a nucleus of a farming operation as well as a dwelling house. Such plots have been referred to as 'tofts'. With the passage of time to the medieval period, many plots within Faknham had barns which in a later period became substantial buildings. Some of these remain to the present day, as is the case with the 'Rectory Barn' now a Fitness Club and the 'Star Barn' which has become the Press Club. Boundaries are extremely persistent features in the landscape, so it is possible to envisage the early land use within the town.

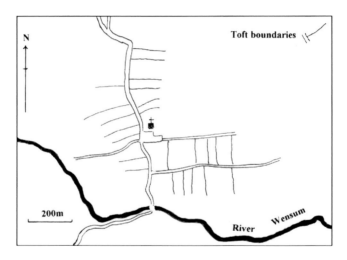

Fig. 9.2. Medieval tofts of Fakenham

As population grew in the early 1200s, the tofts or yards became the site of both houses and small businesses and the yards became known by the person who owned the property. Thus in living memory we had Kerrison's Yard, containing a slaughterhouse which belonged to one of the town's former butchers (now Papworth's). Dunthorne's Yard contained the dairy of Mr Dunthorne who delivered milk by horse-drawn milk float until after the Second World War. Southgate's Yard had the coach-building business of the 19th century which became the motor garage of the 20th century, the site now occupied by Tesco. One yard became the property of the

Methodist Church and was known as Ranters Yard.

Scattered evidence remains of the housing associated with these yards; it consisted of small cottages with a central water pump and outside privy. In the 1930s many of these cottages were declared unsuitable for human habitation and demolished, the people moved into council housing on Jubilee Avenue and King's Road. However, proximity to the town centre and increasing land values and house prices in the last two decades has meant that it became profitable to build new houses in some of the yards. It has also fitted well with schemes to utilise 'grey', run-down or derelict land for beneficial purposes rather than take further 'greenfield' sites for building.

In the mid-1800s William Utting, from an extensive local family, left Fakenham for Walsall where he became a publican and successful builder. In the 1880s he returned to Fakenham with a team of workmen and was responsible for the construction of Walsall Terrace, Birmingham Terrace and Litchfield Street. He also owned the brickworks on Claypit Lane which provided the materials for construction. William Utting is buried in Fakenham cemetery on Queen's Road (Monbiot, 2002).

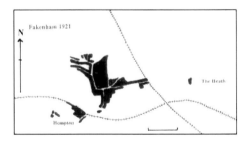

Fig. 9.3. Extent of Fakenham in 1921

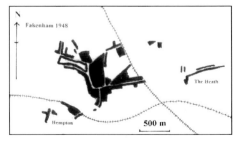

Fig. 9.4. Extent of Fakenham in 1948

The population figures indicate that growth of the town was slow until relatively modern times (Bridges, 2002). The built-up area of Fakenham represented on the 1885 edition of the Ordnance Survey 1: 10,560 (Six Inches to One Mile) map was substantially the same area as that shown on a 1921 map (Fig. 9.3). In the 1920s and 1930s limited expansion of the town occurred in the suburban areas of Wells Road, Hayes Lane, Highfield Road, Holt Road, Jubilee Avenue and The Heath. These areas are included on the plan of the town as it was immediately after the Second World War (Fig. 9.4).

In the 1970s increases in population and new industrial developments began to greatly increase the urban area. The area between Norwich road and Holt road and between Holt road and Greenway lane became urbanised and the formerly isolated hamlet of The Heath became linked to the main settlement. Hempton, which had remained without development expanded on the western side of the Green. The M.& G.N. railway was withdrawn from service in 1959, leaving the L.N.E.R. line with goods services only as shown on Figure 9.5.

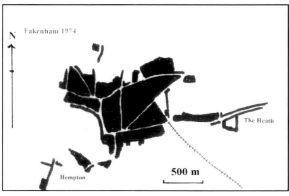

Fig. 9.5. Extent of Fakenham in 1974

Finally, housing development on the northern side of the town, extending as far as Rudham Stile lane, and south of Norwich Road be-tween The Heath and the former railway line considerably increased the built-up area by the millennium. In the east and north-east of the urban area of Fakenham industrial estates provided much needed modern accommodation for new industrial activity. These changes are reflected in the plan of the town in 2000 (Fig. 9. 6).

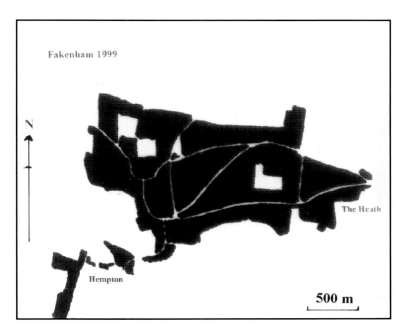

Fig. 9.6. Extent of Fakenham in 2000

References
Bridges, E.M. 2002. The Growth of Fakenham. Fakenham Museum.
Monbiot, R. 2002. The Burnhams Book of Characters and Memories. Rotherfield Management, Burnham Market.

Chapter 10. Fakenham in the 20th Century

Throughout the fist half of the 20th century Fakenham was a fairly self-sufficient little market town with a resident population of about 3,000 people. The town, lying more or less equidistant from Norwich and King's Lynn, was the regional centre for a considerable area of North Norfolk. It was the headquarters of the Walsingham Rural District; it had a magistrates court, police station and crown post office. A limited bus service connected the town with Norwich but did not really compete with the two railway stations which provided more frequent and regular services. Then, as now, the town had its market on Thursdays but it consisted of both a cattle market and the market traders who still come to the town each Thursday.

Fig. 10.1 Fakenham Cattle Market
(Photo Fakenham Local History Society)

A wide range of small shops and services supported the town and surrounding villages. Many of the businesses which had been set up in the previous century survived until relatively recent times. The following is a list of Fakenham businesses culled from a trade almanac of the 1930s (Priest 1932) and from the author's memory, so it is not exhaustive.

Wells Road
Wells Road Post Office; Blake, garage; Edgely, cobbler; Tuthill, builder; Tuthill (Mrs), milliner; Cattle Market Tavern PH; Tuck, baker.

Nelson Road
Harrison, stonemason; Piercy, blacksmith; Nelson PH; Moore, baker.

Oak Street
Broady, butcher; Andrews, hairdresser; George & Balls, blacksmith; Winn, florist; Star PH; Aldred, fish & chips; Hall, pork butcher & greengrocer; Bone, sweets; Dunthorne, milkman; Doctor's surgery; Fox, dentist; Oak PH; Bakers, ladies clothing; Wright, dentist; Kerrison, butcher; Feakes, baker; Southgates, garage; Andrews, woolshop; Powell, saddler & harness maker.

Old Post Office Street
Electricity showroom; Butcher & Andrews, solicitors; Cawdron, wine merchant.

Market Place
Spooner, greengrocer; Whites, wireless; Moore, baker; Stewardsons, stationer & bookseller; Andrews, printer; Aldiss clothing; International Stores, grocer; Bailey Bird, clothing; Red Lion PH; Aldiss, men's outfitter; Wainwright, pianos & music; Powell & Butler, grocer; Café; Holton, chemist; National Provincial Bank; Saunders, men's outfitter; Crown PH; Heyhoe, chemist; Sheringham & Overman, seeds; Barclays Bank; Watson, Dingy & Pope, solicitors; Barnes, greengrocer, White, furnishing & cycles.

White Horse Street
Lancaster Press, printer.

Bridge Street – Hempton Road
Hardware Store, ironmonger; Colls, fishmonger; Burrage, seeds & forrage; Greef & Minster, draper; Keeble, cobbler; Commercial Hotel; Meuse, hairdresser; Oglesby, baker; Rix, leather goods; Bull PH; Massey & Bridges, garage; Dewing & Kersley, millers; Collins & Simpson, tyres; Fakenham Gas Works; M&GN station.

Norwich Street
Pooley, grocer; Long & Beck, auctioneer; Newman, hairdresser, tobacconist & gifts; Bone, clocks & watches; woolshop; Barnhams, electrical goods; Priest, stationery; Parker, jeweller; Brier, fishing tackle; Leech, greengrocer; Printing Works; Cranmer, bookmaker; Stark, seeds & plants; Benson, hair-dresser; Home & Colonial, grocer; Bone, cycles; Meuse, hairdresser; Baker, furnishing; Young, ladies clothing; Universal Supplies, hardware; Chapman, butcher; Windsor café.

Norwich Road
Dugdale, wireless, Bone, photographer; Waterstone, sweets; Carley, garage; Coop, grocer & clothing; Great Eastern PH; LNER Station; Shell oil depot; Dewing, maltings; Richardson, coal & scrap merchant; Harrison, stonemason; Railway Tavern PH; Bell PH.

Holt Road
Main Post Office; Magistrate's Court; Anchor PH; Fakenham Laundry; Baxters, garage; Smith, woodyard; waterworks; Mrs Richardson, corsets; Colman, builder; Duffy, waste materials.

Queens Road
Rampant Horse PH; Needs, garage; telephone exchange.

Cattle Market Street.
Dunthorne antiques; Cattle Market.

Quaker Lane
Howard, motorcycles garage, tyre supplies.

Although some of the enterprises listed had closed before the war, many struggled on, managing to serve the populace with greatly reduced supplies and vital provisions, all of which were rationed throughout the war; some commodities remained rationed until the early 1950s.

The Second World War
Fakenham was a busy place during the war years being surrounded by no less than nine airfields and other military sites. It would have been in the front line had an invasion occurred (Bridges & Baldwin, 2005). Schoolboys practised their French on the Free French airmen who were stationed at nearby airfields and 'got any gum chum' was a phrase used on the Americans who came later. It is now difficult to imagine the construction traffic along the narrow Sculthorpe Road, when the airfield and a new road past it were being built. Needless to say the latter became known as the 'Burma Road' after the infamous Japanese road construction in SE Asia.

A large concrete pill box was built in the market place outside the Red Lion Hotel, now The Bistro; to disguise its true purpose it had a statue placed upon it (Fig. 10.2). Fortunately it never had to be used, and it was so much in the way that it was demolished before the end of the war. Some of its foundations were apparent when the

market place was re-surfaced in the early 2000s. Before that the town pump was in the same position. Although there are drawings of the pump, only a very grainy newspaper illustration remains of the pill box. The location of road blocks on two of the town main roads may still be seen by the numbers painted on the walls of the Postal Sorting Office and near the library in Oak Street.

Fig. 10.2 Wartime pill box
in the Market Place
(Photo Fakenham Local History Society)

95

A static water tank was located in the market place in order to ensure sufficient water for fire-fighting. The civilian population was mobilised to serve in the Home Guard or the Observer Corps as well in the Women's Voluntary Service. Fire-watchers and Air Raid Wardens were appointed and an Air Raid Precautions (ARP) command centre was set up at Baron's Hall. Fakenham had replaced its gas street lighting with electric lights in 1939, just in time for it to be switched off for the blackout which shrouded every part of the country in darkness.

The Observer Corps had an observation post on Hempton Green, near to the Bullock Hills. Sometimes the observers would come home in the morning and say there had been a raid on Norwich and that they could see the glow of the fires in the city.

Fig. 10.3 War damage: the destruction of the Salvation Army Temple
(Photo Fakenham Local History Society)

One day, there was great excitement because a German bomber had dropped a stick of bombs across the town falling in Newman's garden (now Queen's Road car park), the churchyard and the rectory garden. One bomb destroyed the Salvation Army temple (Fig.10.3).

Small boys were intrigued because bones could be seen blown out of the crater in the churchyard. When the siren sounded during school hours children had to go into a bomb shelter which was situated on open ground between the former Infants School and Holt Road.

At the Secondary School, which after the 1944 Education Act became a Grammar School, the teachers were either elderly clergymen or young ladies directly out of the emergency 2-year degree courses put on by the universities during the war. For a time the Secondary School shared their facilities with the Central Foundation School evacuated from the east end of London. There was surprisingly little aggravation between the two sets of school pupils, although the visitors were referred to by the locals as 'Jouls', a non-politically-correct Fakenham schoolboy contraction of 'Jewboys'. The London boys were billeted on local families. The two headmasters shared the same study and lessons were taken at different locations such as the old church hall, then in Wells Road. It must have been a nightmare for Mr Eckersley, the Fakenham Headmaster.

Children had the River Wensum as a swimming pool in summer. The mill pool of Goggs Mill was reasonably deep and had a suitable tree for use as a diving board; it may be remembered that the summers were warmer in the 1940s. In the early years of the war, visits to the seaside were impossible and later, except for a small area facing Wells, the beach was out of bounds with barbed wire and mines, and in any case Wells was a long way away for youngsters to cycle.

The town's industrial expertise was employed to assist the war effort despite losing many men of service age to the forces. With private motoring greatly restricted, motor garages turned their attention to servicing the military vehicles and particularly the vehicles used by contractors in the construction of airfield runway. Massey and Bridges, for example, taught a group of women to make bogie wheels for tanks and bren-gun carriers using the garage's lathes; 12,000 were produced.

As the local town, Fakenham was the place to visit for relaxation. Dances were held at the former drill hall on Holt Road and in the Corn Hall in the Cattle Market. The Central Cinema provided film entertainment in programmes featuring a short B film, the Pathé

News and a feature film. The town's public houses were well patronised. At the end of the war, Fakenham emerged without much damage and without losing too many young men in battle.

Second half of the 20th Century

In the period since the end of World War 2, Fakenham has lost many of its functions. With local government re-organisation in 1974 the town lost out to Cromer as the centre of the North Norfolk District Council. The Council Offices in the former Red Lion on the Market Place were sold. Thus Fakenham lost its 'town hall' in the Market Square which was replaced by a building called 'Fakenham Connect' hidden behind the library. The former Crown Post Office was closed in 1995 and replaced by a counter at the back of a local shop, while the former purpose-built post office is used only as a sorting office. The Police Station was formerly on Gladstone Road in the building that is now the Rectory. A new Police Station was built on Norwich Road together with a Court House, removed from Holt Road. Subsequently, the Magistrate's Court has been closed. A new Fire Station was built on Norwich Road to replace the 1911 building in Hall Staithe. Railway services have been withdrawn: M&GN in 1959 and the LNER in 1969. With the railways went the grain-handling facilities and the maltings on Norwich Road, as well as facilities for handling cattle and sheep. The cattle market closed in 1987 (Fig.10.1)

A new Secondary Modern School was built in 1958-9 and in 1982 was merged with the Grammar School to form the comprehensive High School, and the Sixth-Form College now contains more 17-18 year old pupils than the whole Grammar School had previously. The Grammar School playing field has become Fakenham Cricket Club's ground. Baron's Hall Lawn, for long the home of both Fakenham Football Club (The Ghosts) and the Cricket Club, has been sold for housing. The Ghosts have a new pitch at Clipbush Lane, and the town now has a Rugby Club, situated off Old Wells Road.

Closure of the Co-op on Norwich Road and the construction of a Co-operative supermarket at White Post at the time caused much concern amongst the smaller shopkeepers who could not compete on prices, but this was followed by a Safeway supermarket, now

Morrison's. Together they took considerable trade from the town centre. When Tesco also proposed to build a store in town, the centrally placed Budgen's store closed, and for several months there was no grocery shop in the town centre. Compared with the pre-war days and even the 1950s, the centre of Fakenham has become the province of Banks, Building Societies, House Agents, charity shops, hairdressers, opticians and take-away food shops.

The opening of Tesco in 2007 on the site of the former Edmondson's garage has brought trade back into the centre of town and local shops have reported an increase in trade because there are more people around. The former motor garages, Baxters, Carleys, Edmondsons and Massey and Bridges have all closed to be replaced by larger out-of-town concerns. With the demise of Cox and Wyman's Printing Works in 1982 the opportunity to redevelop the area was taken and a shopping arcade called Miller's Walk was constructed with the former cattle market used as a car park. Some of the railings which formed the animal pens are still present and some of the roof supports from the printing works have been incorporated into Miller's Walk.

Aldiss formerly had a men's outfitters in the Market Place and their main shop in the Upper Market. Several years ago the men's outfitters in the Market Place was amalgamated with the Upper Market shop and a new furniture emporium opened in the redundant printing works building on Old Lane. A branch has opened in Norwich as well. Sadly, as this book is being written the Aldiss management has decided to close the shop in the Upper Market.

Unlike Holt, the town has failed to attract a sufficient number of up-market 'boutique' shops to replace the butchers, bakers and grocers of yesteryear. Consequently, the town centre is now 'scarred' by the presence of closed shops, some of which have been closed for several months and even years. Shopping habits have changed, but this is not the only problem as the choice of shops in the town centre has declined. Small retailers are finding it difficult to make a living and pay the rents demanded by absentee landlords and the business rates levied on shop premises.

The town's urban area has expanded eastwards to engulf The Heath completely and trading estates have been developed. Fakenham Business Park has attracted Volkswagen and Vauxhall garages, a marine engineering firm and a hardware and gardening store. Across the road, Fakenham Industrial Estate has a major haulage company, electrical, heating and plumbing engineers, chemicals, plastics, replacement windows and a wide range of printing enterprises set up by members of the printing trade made redundant by the closure of the printing works. Also in the same part of town food processing has found employment for many people with the Stella Macartney factory, formerly Ross Foods. Back in town on Old Lane the Kinnerton chocolate factory has brought a new enterprise to Fakenham.

Fakenham Racecourse, which has just celebrated its 100th anniversary, has developed considerably during the second half of the 20th century. The facilities have been greatly improved with the Prince of Wales Stand and additional race meetings at intervals throughout the year. The Prince of Wales Stand is also an attractive venue for social functions and a caravan camp and Sports Social Club provide additional attractions so that the site is well used.

References

Baldwin, J. 1982. Fakenham Town on the Wensum. Poppyland, Cromer.

Baldwin, J & Van Damme, E., nd. Another Look at Fakenham. Jim Baldwin Publishing, Fakenham.

Baldwin, J. 1999. Hard Forms & Homework. Fakenham High School & College.

Baldwin, J. & Baldwin, M. 2002. A Good Impression: The Story of Printing in Fakenham. Jim Baldwin Publishing, Fakenham.

Baldwin, J. & Tickle, A. 2007. Memories of Fakenham Lancaster. Revised edition. Jim Baldwin Publishing, Fakenham.

Bridges, E.M. & Baldwin, J. 2005. A Conflict & Memories: Fakenham Remembers World War Two. Fakenham Museum.

Priest, H.H. 1932. Fakenham Almanack and Directory. Fakenham.

Chapter 11. The Churches in Fakenham

Church of England

Christian worship has been practiced in Fakenham since Anglo-Saxon times and even today the most impressive building in the town is the parish church. Christianity was brought to England in AD 597 and the church's following had become widespread by AD 680 when the seat of the northern bishopric in East Anglia was located at North Elmham. Some masonry in the north-east corner of the present Fakenham church is reputed to be part of an original Saxon structure (Anon. nd., and Buckingham, 1971).

No mention of a church is made in the Domesday survey but in the period after the Norman Conquest a stone-built church was erected and it is thought that the doorway at the west end of the north aisle was part of this structure. The present nave and chancel were built in the 14th century followed by the 115 ft high tower in the 15th century. The porch also dates from this period and it was used as a gunpowder store in the early 1600s. Details of the contents are given in the church guide.

The living is held by Trinity College Cambridge and the church is dedicated to the Saints Peter and Paul and it is recorded that the fabric of the building has suffered at times from neglect. In 1597 the chancel was described as 'ruinous and decayed'. At this time the church was thatched, but later restoration work c. 1745 included a lead roof. A thorough restoration occurred in Victorian times, c. 1864, which included a slate roof and introduced the pine pews. The most recent change to the church fabric is the construction of the Trinity Room in the western part of the north aisle. Considerable restoration took place at intervals throughout the 1900s and the work has continued with the re-glazing of the west window and repair of the reredos after the earthquake of 2007.

In the surrounding churchyard, which closed for burials in 1856, the gravestones have been cleared and placed around the edges of what has become St Peter's Garden. In earlier times encroachments took place on the churchyard with the building of shops in Upper Market and in 1860 George Stewardson was permitted to build over the passage to the church from the market place. At the instigation of the Miller Family, a corrugated Mission Hut was constructed on the

Heath. The hut has gone, but the name Mission Lane remains.

Across the river in Hempton, the church of St Stephen formerly stood in a field known as church meadow along the Shereford Road. Its affairs were linked to the Priory which provided services, but with the demise of the priory in 1537, the church was allowed to decay and by 1623 was ruinous. In 1845, a county directory stated that Hempton parishioners had seats in the north aisle of Fakenham Church for which privilege they had to pay 16/- a year to the churchwardens.

In 1856, the Reverend Moxon, a curate at Fakenham, was determined to provide Hempton with its own a church again. It was built upon a plot of land given by Lord Townshend and dedicated to the Holy Trinity. The small church was extended in 1955 using dressed stone from a bomb-damaged Norwich church and other masonry from the original St Stephens, Hempton and from St Margaret's, Pudding Norton (Nicholson, 1977).

After the Reformation there was no church in Fakenham where people of the catholic faith could worship, although some would have attended secret services. In the 19th century a small group began to celebrate mass in a house on Holt Road (1898) but other venues were used, including Wensum House in Hempton where, in 1905, the Bishop gave permission for mass to be said. This state of affairs continued until 1909 when the church of St Anthony of Padua was erected in Wells Road in Fakenham. The church is currently celebrating its centenary.

Independent Churches

Until 1689 the parish church remained the only religious building in Fakenham. In that year, following the Act of Toleration, the Quakers built a meeting House in Quaker Lane. This place of worship was supported by the Peckover family which had settled in Fakenham after the Civil War. Although the meeting house closed for worship around 1800, the building remained in secular use until it was demolished and replaced by a block of flats.

People who did not worship in the established church built their own chapel in Whitehorse Street in 1819. This building still stands and is used now as the Conservative Club; previously it had been the home of the Lancaster Press. In 1895, the Independents, who became known as Congregationalists, built a new chapel for themselves in Norwich Road with the support of the Copeman family from Norwich. This chapel was used until 1958 but the building is now used as an antique centre. Their minister in the mid-19th century was William Legge, an enlightened man who purchased the Fakenham Poor House on The Heath and used it as a theological college. He also supported a Mechanics Institute for the betterment of local men and was instrumental in opening the British School (for dissenters) built in Norwich Road.

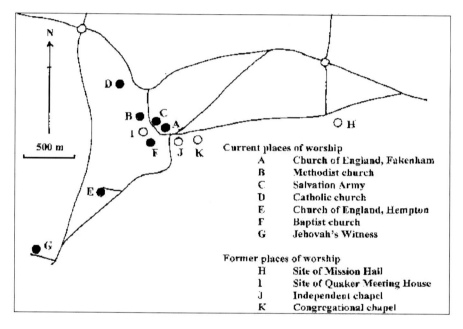

Fig. 11.1 Fakenham Churches

Fakenham's Methodist church began in the independent chapel on White Horse Street. A breakaway group from this chapel became followers of the inspiring preacher John Wesley who visited Fakenham in 1781, but with the departure of the Congregation-alists, further schisms led to the establishment of a Primitive Methodist Church separate from the Wesleyans in Oak Street. The two factions both built chapels in Oak Street, the Wesleyans on the east side, and the Primitives modified a barn, down a yard (Ranter's Yard) on the west side of the road. In January 1908 the foundation stone for a new church, the Buckenham Memorial church was laid and it opened for worship in September of that year. In 1932, the two branches of Methodism re-combined in the new church (Baldwin, 2008).

The Baptists also began life with the independents in the chapel in White Horse Street, but moved to a barn in Swan Street in 1801 which they eventually converted into a church in 1808. Their premises have been modified in 1847, 1869 and 1996.

The Salvation Army came to Fakenham in 1884 and met in the Star Barn on Oak Street. When the former Wesleyan chapel on the east side of the street became vacant they moved in, only to be bombed out during the second world war, after which they returned to the Star Barn until their present building was constructed.

Other denominations are or have been represented in Fakenham. The Plymouth Brethren had a Gospel Hall in White Horse Street between 1880 and the 1960s. The former boys' school in Church Lanes became Kingdom Hall of the Jehovah's Witnesses; subsequently they moved to a new building on the Helhoughton Road in Hempton. A group called the Muggletonians existed from 1657 and may have continued until 1920 (Baldwin and Tickle, 2007).

References
Anon (nd) The Parish Church of SS Peter and Paul Fakenham: a brief history. Fakenham Church PCC, Baldwin.
Baldwin, J. 2008. Wesley's People: the Methodist Heritage of Fakenham. Baldwin Publishing Solutions.
Baldwin, J. and Tickle, A. 2007. Memories of Fakenham Lancaster. Jim Baldwin Publishing Solutions
Buckingham, H. (ed) 1971. The Story of Fakenham and its Church. Fakenham.
FitzJohn, P. 1956. The Story of Hempton. Wyman, Fakenham
Nicholson, N. N, 1977. Hamatuna-Hempton, a village community 1066-1977.

Chapter 12. Local Government

As the centre of a large rural area, Fakenham has been well placed in the past to be a centre for local government. The system of shire counties sub-divided into hundreds and parishes had come into existence even before the Norman Conquest. From Saxon times through to the present day the basic unit of administration has been the parish. The Fakenham parish boundary runs along the River Wensum from Goggs Mill to a point south of The Heath, except where the river has been diverted to Fakenham Mill. Two kilometres downstream from Fakenham Mill the boundary leaves the river in a north-easterly direction, crossing the Norwich Road east of Heath Farm and the Cromer Road before looping around Thorpland to the River Stiffkey which it follows downstream for 1.5 kilometres. From the river the boundary then turns south-west through Water House Farm eventually to take the line of Wells road, Sandy Lane and Goggs' Mill Road to enclose the parish (Fig. 12.1).

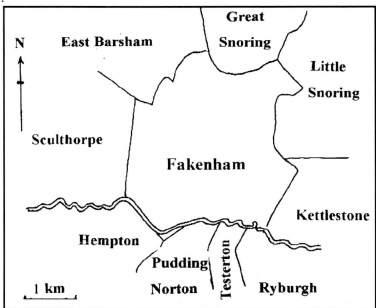

Fig. 12.1 The Parish of Fakenham

A larger historic administrative unit was the hundred. These areas were established before the Norman invasion and may even have originated as earlier tribal territories. According to one source, the hundreds were based upon the ability of a district to provide 100 persons for the purposes of maintenance of law and order. A hundred would be composed of a number of smaller villages and hamlets which were grouped together for administration, law enforcement and defence. The definition of a hundred appears to be based on a human dimension, rather than a geographical area. As the largest settlement within its area, Fakenham was the obvious centre of the Gallow Hundred (Fig. 12.2). Each hundred was administered by a High Constable who was responsible for raising a body of able-bodied men for military service. The High Constable was in turn responsible to the Sheriff of the County.

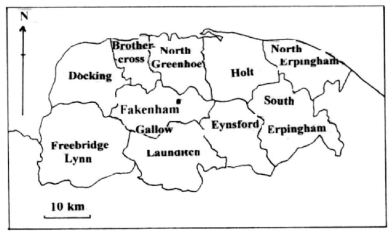

Fig. 12.2 The Hundreds of North Norfolk

However, hundred meetings were not always held in the larger centres but at some convenient central location. The names of the hundreds may give some clues to these meeting places. Did the Gallow Hundred, in which Fakenham is the largest settlement, meet at the site of the Gallows, or was it something to do with the word 'gallus' a plough? In other cases meetings took place at the site of tumuli and this may have given the name ending hoe as in Greenhoe for the hundred in which Wells is situated. The element how or hoe suggests a hill or mound. In the case of the Burnhams, Brothercross Hundred suggests a meeting place at a cross. The hundreds persisted with minor changes until 1834 when a Poor Law Amendment Act brought many of them together based upon the location of the workhouses. Thus the Poor Law Unions were created around the workhouses at Great Snoring, Gressenhall and Docking in the area surrounding Fakenham.

In 1889 County Councils were created within which local affairs were dealt with by Rural District Councils. Fakenham became the centre for the Walsingham Rural District Council (WRDC), one of the fifteen RDCs in Norfolk, with Wells, Cromer, Sheringham and King's Lynn having independent Urban District Councils (Fig.12.3). At different times the offices of the WRDC were in premises in Bridge Street and also at Baron's Hall and the Council was economically run on a small budget raised by the rates.

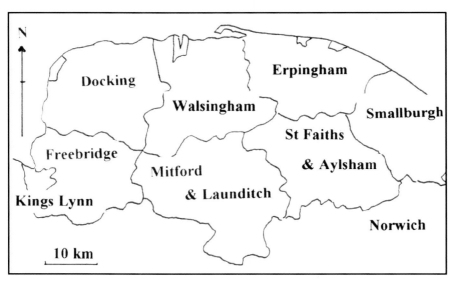

Fig.12.3 The Rural District Councils of North Norfolk before 1974

Finally in 1974, the County of Norfolk was sub-divided into seven District Councils and the Fakenham area was included as part of the North Norfolk District Council (Fig. 12.4). A palatial new district council office was built at Cromer and an ever-increasing number of staff are employed in a bureaucratic operation serving the increasing demands of central government which provides inadequate funds, resulting in escalating local taxation. At the time of writing further local government changes are being put forward, again at substantial cost to the inhabitants with little prospect of better services.

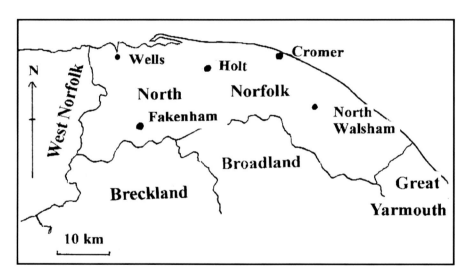

Fig. 12.4 North Norfolk District Council

Fakenham has lost its role as a centre for administration as all decisions of any importance are taken now in the NNDC Offices in Cromer. One cannot but be suspicious that the powers in NNDC regard Fakenham as being at the far end of their district and lower on their scale of priorities compared with the coastal area.

Fakenham has a town council presided over by a mayor but it has limited powers and it struggles to fill the positions upon the Town Council. The councillors serve on three main committees, Leisure and Environment, Development and Markets, and Policy and

Resources. Councilors have control over parks, allotments, playgrounds and cemeteries, planning applications, street lighting, street names, markets and the market tolls fund which can be used for the benefit of institutions in the town. Over the years this fund has benefited many local institutions including the Fakenham Museum.

Postcript – the future

The previous chapters have attempted to bring together the many strands of geology, landscape, pre-history and written history that have led to the existence of the town in which we live. Although it is mostly taken for granted, we have inherited 'our' town from the generations which have gone before. Decisions that they made in their time have moulded the fabric of the town so that the roads we use and buildings we inhabit are all an inheritance from the past. Currently, it is our turn as responsible citizens to continue this process of maintaining the town and to respond to changing circumstances. Fakenham does not exist in isolation and cannot stand still. Like any organism it must grow and develop otherwise it will wither and die. It is perhaps illuminating that one recent report of the town stated that it is a most boring place and another described Fakenham as one of the ten most desirable places in the UK in which to live. Perhaps these contradictory remarks mean we have got it about right!

The District Council is charged with preparing development plans for the future of the town and its surrounding district. These have been prepared by professional planners with appropriate consultation and opportunity for constructive comment by the public. The future development of Fakenham has been examined from the point of view of the role the town currently fulfils, the various issues concerning the physical environment, the community and social life of the town including its economy. These issues highlight the possibility of retaining or changing the various uses to which the land is put in order to achieve the long-term viability of the town.

In the opinion of the District Council's professional planners, Fakenham has the potential to accommodate significant levels of development which would bring with it greater choice of housing and employment, as well as enable increased services to be maintained and developed (NNDC, 2003 & 2006).

Physical Environment
Fakenham is small town in a rural area with a homogeneous population living in attractive and pleasant surroundings. Any further urban expansion should be limited to within the area enclosed by the

northern bypass. The possibility of flooding on the floodplain of the River Wensum has limited urban development on the south side of the town and has left a corridor of low-lying wetlands with semi-natural vegetation and cover for wildlife. The river with the riparian zone is a site of special scientific interest (SSSI) as the Wensum has an aquatic environment uncommon in East Anglia. The possibility of a nature park on the floodplain, extending both east and west of the town, has been suggested and has considerable merit for combined recreation and wildlife conservation. Fakenham Museum is at the centre of the proposed park and with appropriate development could improve greatly the attractiveness of the area for tourism.

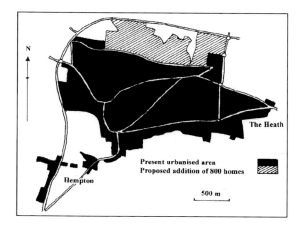

Fig 13.1 Proposals for the extension of Fakenham

Housing

As has been documented in a previous chapter, Fakenham has grown considerably during the past 50 years. Between 2010 and 2021 it is anticipated that a further 1,300 houses will be constructed. Currently, in 2008, around 100 planning permissions have been granted and 830 new dwellings could be built on land between the present northern edge of the town and the A148 by-pass. The planners stress the need for sympathetic development in which a range of housing, a new school, additional medical facilities, increased employment opportunities and provision of open spaces will go hand in hand.

111

Retail provision

Changing patterns of shopping have led to the disappearance of many of the small shops that characterised Fakenham in the middle of the 20th century. Out-of-town supermarkets proved too great a competition for several small retailers. However, once Tesco was established it brought people back into the town centre and the existing small food shops, such as the bakeries and the greengrocery have survived. Proposals for additional shops and living accommodation in the Bridge Street area, have again been put forward in 2009 despite being rejected by a town meeting a few years ago. The shop premises in Norwich Street were constructed some 200 years ago and no longer meet the requirements of modern merchandising, being small, often on different levels and poorly lit. Although attempts have been made to provide a boutique style of shop in these premises, there has not been the success seen in Holt. By contrast the Miller's Walk shops are modern units within an arcade which is made secure at night. High rent and rates are a problem for retailers and currently some shops are empty. The planners propose that an additional 4,000 to 8,600m^2 is to be made available for shop premises between now and 2016 to meet the demands of an increased population.

With a current population of about 9,000 the town cannot support a wide range of small retail businesses in competition with supermarkets and so there is a narrow range of shops, dominated by banks, house agents and charity shops. The town still attracts people from villages in a wide surrounding area on Thursdays for its market. Although the buying and selling of crops and animals has ceased and trade in agricultural products and necessities is no longer tied to a market day, the market traders still have 50 to 60 stalls which offer a wide range of products including clothing, foodstuffs, flowers and plants, art works and stationery.

Several fast-food outlets, four cafés, four banks, three house agents, four hairdressers, three opticians, two antique shops, two chemists, two furniture shops, two jewellers, two dress shops, a shoe shop, two mobile phone shops and a white goods shop form the nucleus of retail trade. The picture is fluid as the pressure of ever-increasing rents, rising council tax (and an international currency crisis) make trading difficult for small individual shopkeepers. For the future, the planned increase in the population will help to support an increased number and quality of shops and attract more people to shop in the town centre. It would greatly help if the town's car parks were made free (as in Dereham) because the current charges are a deterrent, forcing customers out of town, but this decision is out of Fakenham's control.

Employment

In June 2003, the District Council described the situation in Fakenham as being one of low unemployment and relatively buoyant economy. The District Council still expressed confidence in 2006 when it backed a comprehensive retail development in the area of Bridge Street car park and in the areas on either side of White Horse Street. There is still space available on the areas designated for light industrial activity. Pious hopes are expressed for more highly skilled and better paid jobs as well as improved opportunities for youngsters.

Tourism

Fakenham is situated just inland of the North Norfolk Area of Outstanding Natural Beauty. It has even been described as the gateway to the North Norfolk Coast. The main roads, A148 and A1065, efficiently bypass the town, but for the future the planners suggest improved signs to the town centre and by implication to the town's visitor attractions, none of which are officially signed at present. With hotels and B & B houses for overnight stays, several cafés and pubs for refreshment, an attractive parish church and a unique Museum of Gas and Local History, the town should be given a higher profile for visiting tourists. Just out of town are the nature reserves of Pensthorpe and Sculthorpe Fen, both of which are well worth a visit from locals and tourists alike. A caravan touring site forms part of the Fakenham Racecourse complex at Pudding Norton.

Travellers

In 2008, despite strong protestations from the townsfolk, an £800,000 gypsy encampment was imposed upon Fakenham even though there is but slight demand in this area from the travelling community. National government has dictated that provision must be made, placing the Local District Council in the invidious position of having to go against local wishes in an undemocratic manner.

Community Facilities

Formal community facilities exist in the town including the Community Centre which has a large hall and some subsidiary rooms. Responsibility for upkeep is divided and criticism is levelled at its layout. A multi-use sports facility has been opened adjacent to the High School and another sports centre is located on the Racecourse. Hempton village Memorial Hall and various church halls provide meeting places for local societies. Considerable support exists for the construction of a swimming pool and a skateboard park but, as other communities have found, a swimming pool is costly to maintain. Several local walks have been formalised by the local authority and itineraries for these walks are available at the Museum. These could be extended to link the nature reserves to east and west of the town.

Fakenham Museum, as well as being a museum for the coal gas industry of pre-natural gas days, is also the centre for various local history activities and for the Community Archives. It is hoped to expand the facilities for local history on the site in the near future. Adult Education facilities in the town have been cut back in the last few years and only limited courses of a vocational nature are provided.

The existing recreation ground on Queen's Road has had a troubled history of vandalism and attempts are being made to revitalise the area and make provision for youngsters. A new park or public open space is suggested for land on the north side of Barber's lane in an area surrounded by housing. An area to the east of the Museum on the south side of the river forms the Aldiss Community Park. Like the Queen's Road recreation ground, it has suffered from vandalism. Attempts to make it a pleasant place are constantly confounded and hopefully, if the proposal for a larger public open space on the floor of the Wensum valley goes ahead, the area will be upgraded and become more attractive.

Transport

Fakenham is reasonably well served by buses with local services to Norwich, King's Lynn, Cromer, Dereham and London but there is no direct bus connection to Stansted Airport. Bus services do not operate in the evenings. There is also a local bus service across the town. British Rail services to Fakenham ceased many years ago, but railway enthusiasts would like to extend the former LNER line from Wymondham and Dereham to Fakenham, which is conceivable. An even more ambitious plan is for an orbital railway which would make a circuit from Norwich utilising the old M&GN track bed and along the old LNER track-bed back to Norwich. This may take longer to achieve.

Route No.1 of the Sustrans national cycle path passes right through the centre of Fakenham. It should not be difficult to encourage and provide for more cycling visitors in the future. Plans for increased local facilities for cyclists, linking the residential areas and the recreational areas in and around the town are proposed.

Health Care

In the 1930s Fakenham held carnival parades to raise money for a cottage hospital, but it all came to nought. At last, in recent times nursing care has been provided at Cranmer House, but this was drastically reduced in 2008 by the Health Authority when common sense suggests an expansion of nursing care will be required by a growing town with an ageing population. Hospital patients in the Fakenham area face hour-long journeys either to Norwich or King's Lynn at their own expense often for only a ten-minute appointment.

The Fakenham Medical Practice cares for ailments in its surgery and in local villages including Walsingham, where there is another surgery. The practice is staffed by eleven general practitioners and several nurses. Despite these numbers of medical staff, the abrogation of after-hours medical care to agencies has been disastrous with many complaints. The surgery is also the location for paramedic emergency services. With the proposed growth of the town, increased medical facilities will be required and are currently under discussion.

A few months ago, the author stopped for refreshment in a small town of similar size to Fakenham in a neighbouring county. There was nowhere to purchase a cup of tea and virtually all its shops were boarded up or empty. Thoughts turned to home and I earnestly hoped that Fakenham would not suffer in the same way as a result of changed patterns of administration and shopping habits. In compiling this account of Fakenham at the beginning of the 21st century I am optimistic that the town I have known since childhood will continue to flourish.

References

North Norfolk District Council (NNDC), 2003. Whole Settlement Strategy, Fakenham. Cromer.

North Norfolk District Council (NNDC), 2006. Settlement Leaflet, Fakenham. Cromer.

Index